The Left Case Against the EU

The Left Case Against the EU

Costas Lapavitsas

polity

The right of Costas Lapavitsas to be identified as Author of this Work has been
asserted in accordance with the UK Copyright, Designs and Patents Act 1988.

First published in 2019 by Polity Press

Reprinted 2018 (three times), 2019 (twice)

Polity Press
65 Bridge Street
Cambridge CB2 1UR, UK

Polity Press
101 Station Landing
Suite 300
Medford, MA 02155, USA

ISBN-13: 978-1-5095-3105-9
ISBN-13: 978-1-5095-3106-6 (pb)

A catalogue record for this book is available from the British Library.
Library of Congress Cataloging-in-Publication Data

Names: Lapavitsas, Costas, 1961- author.
Title: The left case against the EU / Costas Lapavitsas.
Description: Medford : Polity Press, [2018] | Includes bibliographical
   references and index.
Identifiers: LCCN 2018020994 (print) | LCCN 2018040086 (ebook) | ISBN
   9781509531080 (Epub) | ISBN 9781509531059 (hardback) | ISBN 9781509531066
   (pbk.)
Subjects: LCSH: Political parties--European Union countries. |
   Neoliberalism--European Union countries. | Right and left (Political
   science)--European Union countries. | Ideology--European Union countries.
   | Sovereignty.
Classification: LCC JN50 (ebook) | LCC JN50 .L37 2018 (print) | DDC
   341.242/2--dc23
LC record available at https://lccn.loc.gov/2018020994

Typeset in 11 on 14 pt Sabon by
Servis Filmsetting Ltd, Stockport, Cheshire
Printed and bound in Great Britain by TJ International Ltd, Padstow, Cornwall

The publisher has used its best endeavours to ensure that the URLs for external
websites referred to in this book are correct and active at the time of going to press.
However, the publisher has no responsibility for the websites and can make no guarantee that a site will remain live or that the content is or will remain appropriate.

Every effort has been made to trace all copyright holders, but if any have been over-
looked the publisher will be pleased to include any necessary credits in any subsequent
reprint or edition.

For further information on Polity, visit our website: politybooks.com

Contents

Contents

Figures

vii

Acknowledgements

Several people should be thanked for making this book possible without bearing any responsibility for its shortcomings. Fritz Scharpf and Wolfgang Streeck provided intellectual testing and support during a brief stay in Cologne. Particular thanks should go to Martin Höpner, who, apart from being a sharp interlocutor, went through the text meticulously and with a critical eye. Bob Brenner spent time and effort examining some of the key arguments. Stergios Skaperdas has long been an invaluable port of call to discuss economic and political ideas. Makoto Itoh read the text and made comments with his usual sagacity. C.J. Polychroniou, Paul O'Connell, and Agustín Menéndez also made useful suggestions. George Owers read the text thoroughly and helped give it its final form. Reference should be made to Thanos Moraitis, Giorgos Diagourtas, and Alkim Kiziltug for help with obtaining materials as well as commenting on the content. Finally, Dimitris Argyroulis read the text carefully and made helpful comments on the content and on the bibliography.

1

The European Union
and the Left

Fragmentation and retreat of democracy

The European Union currently finds itself in a state of profound and uncommon instability. To be sure, the EU has also faced difficulties in the past. After the global economic shocks of the 1970s, for instance, in its previous incarnation as the European Economic Community, it lost direction and went through a period of drift. But the instability of the 2010s is of a different order because it is rooted in economic malfunctioning and has become political. The ideological authority of the EU has shrivelled, its democratic credentials have been devalued, its moral standing has taken a series of blows, and its unity has cracked. In 2016, following a bitterly contested referendum, Britain decided to leave. Moreover, rising right-wing and authoritarian parties in several other countries have begun to pose a direct challenge to the very existence of the EU.

The previous three decades had been very different. In the early 1980s the EEC shook off the torpor of the 1970s and expanded by admitting Greece, Spain, and Portugal. More than the formal accretion of new members, however, it engaged in organizational, institutional, and ideological expansion signalled by the strong presence of the European Commission, led by Jacques Delors. A series of crucial steps were taken, including the Single European Act, signed in 1986, and the Maastricht Treaty of 1992.[1] Further economic and political integration appeared to be the order of the day, and the old appellation of the EEC was superseded.

The Maastricht Treaty came hard on the heels of the collapse of the Eastern Bloc and the reunification of Germany. It was very much a product of its time marked by the discrediting of state-controlled socialism, the retreat of organized labour in the previous decade in the face of Margaret Thatcher and Ronald Reagan, and the ascendancy of neoliberal economics in both theory and policy. That was the moment of Francis Fukuyama's *The End of History and the Last Man*, a book that gained tremendous visibility by claiming that liberal democracy and free-market capitalism went hand-in-hand, and together had actually won the grand historical contest among political and social systems.[2] The Maastricht Treaty encapsulated the spirit of the time for Europe, and was a moment of historic importance in the evolution of the European project.[3]

The EU engaged in further sustained expansion in the 1990s and the 2000s, above all by incorporating a host of new countries in Eastern Europe and developing its international presence. The union lacked an army and had no real foreign policy, but it was an economic giant that had largely eliminated internal barriers to trade and the movement of capital. It was, moreover, in command of a form of money that competed against the dollar as an international reserve. Institutionally it possessed a vast array of laws backing the transnational presence of the European Court of Justice. It also had a complex administrative machinery, with a powerful Commission and a European Parliament, employing a large bureaucracy, mostly in Brussels. The image that the EU increasingly sought to project during those decades was of 'soft power' – a beacon of democracy, individual rights, and social protection. A novel political entity appeared to have been created in Europe, a monument to solidarity and peace after the bloodbaths of the twentieth century, which seemed to combine political liberalism and economic neoliberalism.[4]

The global crisis of 2007–9 and, even more, the Eurozone crisis of 2010–12 have left that image in tatters. The response of the EU to the crisis pointed to cold calculation rather than solidarity as its operating principle. Sharply hierarchical power structures and hegemonic behaviour made themselves acutely felt within the union. The paramount objective was to rescue the common currency, the euro, for its collapse would have delivered a mortal blow to the structures built after the Maastricht Treaty. The costs of this rescue were imposed overwhelmingly on the weakest member states.

The measures taken and the policies implemented throughout this period were determined by professional politicians and technocratic experts inhabiting the core institutions of the union. A pronounced 'depoliticization' of economic and social policies took place, a process that had actually begun much earlier, as is evident, for example, in the old debate on the 'crisis of representation', but emerged with ruthless clarity during the global economic crisis.[5] The forms of democracy were generally observed, with active parliaments and a free press, but only the wilfully blind would claim that the content of democracy was also honoured. And even the forms of democracy were frequently side-lined as the letter and the spirit of the law were by-passed by emergency measures.

National electorates were allowed to vote for any party they wanted as long as the same array of economic and social policies were adopted in the end. Parliamentary debate visibly shrunk across Europe, and privately owned newspapers and television channels practised astonishing self-censorship. Big business and big banks, hiring an army of lobbyists, set the political agenda in member states and in Brussels. Formal politics became increasingly remote for great swathes of people, especially wage workers and the poor, the self-employed and the owners of small businesses. Liberal democracy was gradually hollowed out in Europe, and the blame for that lay squarely with liberal democracy itself.[6]

The hollowing out of democracy was perceived by the plebeian classes of Europe as a loss of sovereignty. Conceited specialists often imagine that the poor neither appreciate nor understand sovereignty. It is indeed true that the finer nuances of international law, or the rights of states over land, sea, and air, or the more obscure clauses of international treaties are the preserve of experts. But popular sovereignty is immediately and directly understood by the plebeian strata because it means having a say on the conditions of life in the neighbourhood, the local community, the town, and the city. And insofar as popular sovereignty stretches in practice over the mechanisms determining national economic and social policies, it blends perceptibly into national sovereignty. The lower classes are not fooled when external forces shape national tax, tariff, subsidy, credit, and money policies.

The plebeian classes of Europe were right to perceive the hollowing out of democracy as a loss of sovereignty, for democracy is an integral part of popular sovereignty and extends far beyond the mere ability to vote periodically. It naturally translates into the ability of the poor, the workers, the self-employed, and others to have influence over their conditions of life. That, however, requires appropriate political structures, and liberal democracy has always been deficient in facilitating plebeian participation in social life. As its mechanisms and institutions were hollowed out in Europe during the last few decades, an unprecedented sense of powerlessness came to prevail among the poor.

The sense of powerlessness was inseparable from the further economic marginalization of the lower social classes during the same period. In old-fashioned and perfectly apposite Marxist terms, the decline of democracy and the loss of popular sovereignty in Europe reflect a historic shift in favour of capital and against labour. For labour this shift has amounted to a tremendous escalation of insecurity with regard to employment, income, medical care, pensions, and so forth. For capital it has meant the rapacious appropriation of national wealth, propelling inequality to levels unprecedented in the post-war years. The policies of the EU to confront the Eurozone crisis have further favoured capital while worsening the conditions of labour.

Against this background of economic and political malfunctioning, the trigger for political turbulence was the refugee and migrant crisis of the 2010s. Relatively free movement of workers within the EU after the Treaty of Maastricht significantly increased immigrant populations in several countries. Britain in particular acquired a sizeable layer of Eastern European workers. During the same period immigration across the Mediterranean, mostly by young men from Africa, exerted a steady pressure. The scales were tipped in 2015 by waves of desperate families displaced by civil war in Syria and seeking refuge in Europe in 2015. The actual numbers involved were not enormous, and compared to the aggregate population and the gross domestic product (GDP) of the EU they would never have justified the term 'crisis'. But a crisis it became as EU mechanisms proved incapable of handling the flows, and aimed to prevent refugees and migrants from reaching core countries, where most wanted to go. The result was that safe passage was denied to helpless people, forcing them to seek ever more perilous ways of reaching Western Europe and often paying with their lives. The Mediterranean became a graveyard for thousands.

The refugee and migrant crisis catalysed political developments in Europe. Ultra-conservative forces found amenable terrain on which to manufacture imaginary threats about hordes of foreigners invading the continent. Identity and cultural issues were thrown into the pot as Islam was portrayed as the historic enemy of Christian Europe. The Far Right began to speak the language of sovereignty and security for the people of Europe. It opposed the EU and rejected liberal democracy in favour of authoritarianism, even when it formally complied with electoral practices. Political barbarism raised its head within the EU to take advantage of the forces of fragmentation.

The European Union and the Left

The challenge for the Left

For the Left these tribulations posed a host of political, ideological, and moral issues of the first order. The relationship with the EEC and subsequently the EU has been a hotly contested issue within the Left for several decades, but the change in the dominant attitude during recent decades has been nothing short of astonishing.[7] The most dramatic change has taken place in the United Kingdom. Suffice it only to mention that when Britain joined the EEC in 1973 – and held a referendum in 1975 on the terms of joining which saw a majority in favour – the strongest opposition was to be found in the Labour Party and the trades unions. The EEC was perceived by the Left as a capitalist club that would harm workers' interests and damage British sovereignty.

The sea change in the attitude of the European Left has its roots in the failure of the Mitterrand government in France in 1981.[8] Elected on a radical ticket of economic and social transformation, François Mitterrand was unable to sustain expansionary Keynesian policies in the face of opposition by banks and other established interests, which generated downward pressures on the French franc. His Finance Minister, Jacques Delors, was quick to draw the conclusion that the future of social democratic policies lay with the EEC, rather than with the nation states of Europe.

Delors, who became President of the European Commission in 1985, played a crucial role in the creation and expansion of the EU in the 1990s, and promoted the Social Chapter of workers' rights and social protection, which is often deployed as evidence that the EU is fundamentally a progressive force. The collapse

7

of the Eastern Bloc and the consequent discrediting of socialism and communism in the early 1990s settled the issue for much of the Left in Europe, and especially for social democrats. The belief arose that social progress was only possible within the framework of the EU. By the 2000s even a figure like Toni Negri, whose political origins were anything but social democratic, fervently argued that the EU would overcome the constraints of the nation state and provide a counterweight to ruthless US capitalism.[9]

It is, thus, no surprise that EU turmoil in the 2010s has reawakened sharp divisions within the Left, most prominently with regard to the European Economic and Monetary Union (EMU) and its common currency, the euro.[10] These divisions have been spurred by the relentless ascendancy of neoliberalism in the EU since its creation after Maastricht. Neoliberalism is an ideology that is hard to define accurately, but is unmistakable in its presence.[11] It is marked by a strong belief in the merits of free markets and private enterprise, coupled with an equally strong antipathy toward the public sector, collective agents, and organized labour. The common currency, which steadily became the pre-eminent institutional structure of the EU, has abetted the rise of neoliberalism and entirely deflated the social democratic spirit of Delors' Social Chapter.

Divisions within the Left were also spurred because the development of the EU, far from promoting convergence, actually generated new forces of divergence in Europe. A core has emerged in the EU comprising France, the Netherlands, Austria, Italy (which also has a foot outside the core), and other countries, among which Germany enjoys a hegemonic ascendancy. The core is matched by several peripheral groupings, for instance the Baltic countries, or various combinations of Balkan countries. However, two groupings – quite distinct from each other – stand out and point to the future direction of Europe. The first is the Southern periphery, entirely within the EMU, and comprising Spain, Portugal, and Greece. The second is the Central European periphery, comprising Poland, the Czech Republic, Hungary, Slovakia, and Slovenia, with the last two belonging to the EMU.

The ascendancy of Germany has further led to new political forms and institutional arrangements in the EU. The defining moment arrived when Germany assumed leadership vis-à-vis its European partners in determining the EU response to the crisis of the 2010s. It accomplished this feat by taking advantage of its position as prime European creditor, built up over years of industrial supremacy and exporting surpluses. It obliged debtor countries to accept suffocating policies of austerity and market liberalization as the condition for bailing them out. It also imposed changes across the EU that have institutionalized austerity and neo-liberalism. Lest it be misunderstood, however, German hegemony remains conditional on a host of factors that require constant institutional rebalancing and compromise within the EU.

The neoliberal and hegemonic transformation of the EU has been a matter of considerable analytical concern in the academic world.[12] It has also been a source of great political anxiety within the declining ranks of the social democrats. More broadly within the Left the dominant current is unwilling to acknowledge that the outbreak of the Eurozone crisis, as well as the ensuing regime of austerity and liberalization, have been induced by the very structure of the EU, and especially by the EMU. Instead, these developments are viewed more generically as expressing the prevalence of neo-liberalism across mature capitalist countries leading to maldistribution of income and weak demand followed by predictable government attempts to tackle the problems in the interests of capital and at the expense of labour. The conclusion thus drawn is that the Left should wage a counter-attack on neoliberalism by fighting for concrete policies to strengthen labour against capital as well as fostering transnational unity. Often this view is coupled with a demand for 'More Europe', that is, for stronger integration, or for a push in the direction of federalism, on the assumption that the lurch of the EU in a neoliberal direction was facilitated by the incompleteness of the union.[13]

From this perspective, the EMU and the EU are considered, at bottom, as arenas in which to fight political struggles. Neoliberal and anti-working-class policies, far from being inherent in the institutional functioning of the EMU and the EU, are seen as merely reflecting the transient balance of class forces in key countries, such as Germany and France. Calls to exit or dissolve the EMU, in this view, would not only be pointless, but could also open a path for siding with right-wing nationalist and authoritarian forces. The political conclusion drawn is that the Left ought to separate the mechanisms of the EMU and the EU from their neoliberal political baggage, thus allowing the same mechanisms to promote national and working-class solidarity across Europe. For much of the European Left it is an article of faith that the EMU and the EU should be defended in the name of internationalism, while being criticized for their neoliberal policies.

Nothing could be more misleading than this perspective. The EU and the EMU are not a neutral set of governing bodies, institutions, and practices that could potentially serve any socio-political forces, parties, or governments, with any political agenda, depending on their relative strength. Rather, they are structured in the interests of capital and against labour. They have also gradually become geared to serving the economic advantages, and thereby the international agenda, of a particular dominant class, above all, German industrial export capitalists.

Given this overriding reality, to hope that the outlook of the EMU and the EU could be altered through the simultaneous election of left-wing governments in core countries, drawing upon common anti-neoliberal policies and supported by grass-roots workers' movements, is to add fantasy to misunderstanding. The political emptiness of this view was made clear in 2015 by the failure of the left-wing SYRIZA government in Greece.

The EU and the EMU are beyond left-wing reform, and probably beyond major structural reform altogether. Confronted with the tendency of the EU toward fragmentation and the rise of right-wing authoritarianism, the Left needs to propose fresh policies capable of tilting the balance of power toward labour, strengthening democracy, recouping sovereignty, and providing a feasible socialist perspective for the continent. For that to become a political reality, however, the Left must recapture its historic radicalism and reject the mechanisms of the EMU and the EU, including to the point of exit.

On that basis it could in practice defend the rights of citizens and migrants, while assuaging frictions and tensions among European nations. The rest of this book considers and develops these arguments.

2

The Evolution of the EU: From Maastricht to Now

Neoliberalism and hegemony in the EU – drawing on Hayek

The Maastricht Treaty of 1992 proved crucial to the evolution of the European project. The Treaty was the fruit of long negotiation and debate, and its most important provision was the creation of the common currency, the euro. It also reasserted the 'Four Freedoms of the EU', which were already stipulated in the original Treaty of Rome of 1957 in relation to the EEC, namely the free movement of goods, the free movement of capital, the free establishment and provision of services, and the free movement of persons. Maastricht wrought fundamental changes to the European project compared to the first decades of its existence, not least by favouring the reinterpretation of the Four Freedoms as individual rights, and thus allowing them to be used against collective interests and policies.

From the 1950s to the 1970s the EEC functioned as an alliance created at the peak of the Cold War – with the support of the USA – which provided a further bulwark against the USSR in Europe. It was essentially a customs union coupled with a pact for the promotion of the coal and steel industries and the protection of Western European agriculture. Transnational institutions were created, including the European Parliament, the Commission, and so on, but during those years the nation state retained tremendous power to intervene in the domestic economies of member states, and to promote welfare policies.[1] That was the time of the long post-war boom, a unique period in the history of capitalism marked by rapid growth, rising incomes, and declining inequality.

Maastricht came after the long boom was well and truly over, following the great global crises of the 1970s and the dramatic political and social retreat of labour in the 1980s. True to the new spirit of the times, the Treaty aimed to support the single European market, above all by providing a single currency, the euro. The single market and the euro together supplied the impetus for a further push toward European integration under the umbrella of the EU.

In the years following Maastricht neoliberalism has come to dominate the EU, and we do not need to go far to identify the root causes of this development. In a prescient essay written in 1939, Friedrich Hayek, the intellectual father of neoliberalism, spelled out the likely consequences of 'Interstate Federalism' in Europe.[2] Hayek, who was broadly sympathetic to the idea of a European federation, argued that a federal union would necessarily remove the impediments to the free movement of 'men, goods, and capital'. The union would become a 'single market' and therefore prices and wages would tend to reflect production costs and living conditions across member states, avoiding arbitrary divergences imposed by state authorities. Releasing the price system from externally imposed divergences would give a decisive boost to what Hayek called 'liberalism', or, more accurately for our purposes, neoliberalism.

It is instructive to follow Hayek's reasoning closely in this connection. Hayek claimed that a federal union would have to put in place a framework to ensure the free movement referred to above, thus greatly reducing the scope for economic intervention by each member state in four respects.[3] First, it would become impossible for member states to apply domestic policies favouring particular industries or economic sectors by fixing the price of inputs, output, and labour. Second, member states would not be able to adopt an independent monetary policy, and indeed the union would probably have to form its own central bank. Third, it would be much more difficult for member states to intervene and control economic activity by regulating the quality of goods and the practices of work. Fourth, the methods of raising revenue through tax would become more homogeneous to prevent the outflow of capital from one member state to another.

A federal union, in short, would inevitably restrict the ability of each member state independently to intervene in the sphere of the economy, thus bolstering 'liberalism'. It might be objected, however, that the union as a whole could step into the shoes of the weakened member states, thereby delivering the interventionist policies made impossible for individual states. Hayek dismissed this objection for reasons based mostly on the efficacy of tariffs, but his argument is easily applicable to other forms of government policy, and is worth exploring somewhat further.[4]

For Hayek, any tariff that protected a particular industry would have to be based on a nationalist ideology making the tariff acceptable to the parts of society that bore its costs in the form of higher prices and restricted access to imported goods. A federal union as a whole could not possess any such nationalist ideology. Thus, Hayek thought that, if a tariff was introduced, some member states would support it but others would refuse to accept it. More broadly, any form of industrial policy that defended a particular economic sector would fall prey to the same reactions, as long as there was sufficient variation of economic conditions among member states. Policies on working hours, unemployment insurance, and working conditions would be similarly affected.[5] For Hayek, the union would inevitably veer toward the lowest common denominator with regard to tariffs, industrial policy, labour market policy, and other forms of state intervention. Otherwise member states would not accept the union itself.

Since both the weakened individual member states and the federal union as a whole would be unable to intervene forcefully in economic activity, it followed that there would be 'less government all round if the federation is to be practicable'.[6] Even more strongly, the union would probably have to delegate aspects of economic policy to local and regional units of power, and it would have to police and enforce the compliance of member states with free movement to prevent individual states from bypassing agreed terms through administrative interventions.

In sum, for Hayek, a European federation would be a decisive step toward encouraging and enforcing 'liberalism' in economic life:

> In a federation economic policy will have to take the form of providing a rational permanent framework within which individual initiative will have the largest possible scope and will be made to work as beneficently as possible; and it will have to supplement the working of the competitive mechanism where, in the nature of the case, certain services cannot be brought forth and be regulated by the price system.[7]

Indeed the union might prove the last resort and the true abode of 'liberalism' in a world full of illiberal forces:

> [W]hen, even within these [liberal] democracies, the socialists are becoming steadily more nationalist and the nationalists steadily more socialist, is it too much to hope for a rebirth of real liberalism, true to the ideal of freedom and internationalism and returned from its temporary aberrations into the nationalist and the socialist camps? The idea of interstate federation as the consistent development of the liberal point of view should be able to provide a new *point d'appui* for all those liberals who have despaired of and deserted their creed during the periods of wandering.[8]

Hayek's analysis posited the neoliberal evolution of a European federation as a necessary outcome of the drive toward integration. His essay was not a prescriptive statement regarding the desired path of an interstate federation but an analysis of the internal development of a federation aiming to create a single market. For Hayek, once the single market was in place, the only feasible direction of movement would be toward 'liberalism', and in this respect his thinking has been largely confirmed. That is not to say, however, that the neoliberal evolution of the EU has fully borne out Hayek's analysis.

For one thing, the EU has failed to develop strong federal structures in defence and foreign policy, both of which were considered by Hayek to be prominent and legitimate aims of an interstate federation.[9] For another, the EU has created mountains of legislation – the *acquis communautaire* – through various Treaties, Regulations, Directives, and Decisions, the function of which has generally been to promote neoliberalism. This legislation has also allowed the EU to intervene across several economic and social fields – environmental protection, consumer rights, labour rights, social rights, and so on. For yet another thing, the EU has gone far beyond a 'common monetary policy', not least by creating the EMU and the euro, to which Hayek objected when they were proposed in the 1970s, as shall be seen below. Attached to the common currency is the Stability and Growth Pact, reinforced through an array of legal and institutional changes since 2010, which monitors the fiscal policies of member states in ways that far exceed Hayek's mild fiscal strictures with regard to generating tax income.

Important in this respect is the principle of 'subsidiarity', enshrined at Maastricht, which basically postulates that EU action takes precedence over that of member states only when it is more effective at the national, regional, or local level. 'Subsidiarity' is tied up with 'proportionality', which requires that any action by the EU should merely extend to what is necessary to achieve the objectives of EU Treaties. In practice these principles have created a contested terrain between the

EU and member states. The corresponding legislation of nation states tends to be subsumed under that of the EU, but the balance is delicate and always depends on political prerogatives. In the refugee crisis, for instance, national legislation in practice prevailed over EU legislation, as will be seen briefly in subsequent chapters.

The EU, despite its neoliberal turn, has not become the federal 'liberal' structure that Hayek envisaged.[10] It possesses the power to shape the actions of nation states, but remains a treaty-based alliance, all the members of which retain the power to influence its institutions. It is a transnational juggernaut haphazardly thrown together and rolling in a neoliberal direction.

The relevant academic literature casts some light on this development. A strong current of 'intergovernmentalists' consider the union to be a set of interstate, or intergovernmental, institutions that do not fundamentally challenge the sovereignty of each nation state.[11] Governments of member states, it is asserted, have opted to share sovereignty with the aim of achieving specific objectives, especially in the economic field. According to this current, the direction of the EU is determined less by supranational institutions – the European Parliament, the European Commission, the European Court of Justice – and more by national governments that respond to domestic political pressures in the first instance. Another current are the 'neo-functionalists', who consider that European integration depends on supranational bodies that have a vested interest in furthering integration. Nation states accept integration because cooperating in certain fields is beneficial, and this in turn promotes further cooperation.[12] The steady advance of economic integration has led to sovereignty draining away from nation states toward supranational bodies that deal with concrete issues, and that are the driving force of the EU. Both currents are agreed that supranational institutions have become more powerful over time. However, the 'intergovernmentalists' argue that the delegation of power to supranational institutions, and indeed the general exercise of power by the EU, remains under the active or latent control of member states. The 'neo-functionalists', on the other hand, claim that there is a self-reinforcing dynamic which gives supranational institutions the strength to push for EU integration that goes even further than member states would want.[13]

The actual development of the EU has been far more complex than a putative opposition between weakening nation states and strengthening union. EU member states are also capitalist states, and class relations are fundamental to their make-up as well as to their interactions. The resilience of the nation state in Europe is linked to maintaining the balance of class relations in each country, thus requiring command over the structures of judicial, military, administrative, and other power. Class relations mark the interactions of each member state with the union but also among member states, determining the interests that are to be defended and promoted. In relations among EU member states it has always been easier to detect hierarchy and power rather than solidarity and partnership.

In the course of the Eurozone crisis it became clear that sovereignty has not drained away from individual member states to remotely the same degree. The EU is not simply a political body – 'intergovernmentalist' or 'neo-functional' – that generates mutual benefits and is jointly supported by all member states. Power and domination run through its transnational institutions, as has been nakedly manifested in the past decade. The ascendancy of neoliberal ideology since Maastricht has coincided with the hegemonic ascendancy of Germany in the institutions of the EU, matched by a growing divergence among member states. German hegemony is conditional on the transnational nature of the EU, and three factors are paramount in this respect.

The first is that German hegemony rests on an array of EU economic institutions, above all the common currency. It is not the economic strength of German capital per se that has made the country hegemonic, but its economic strength within the institutional framework of the EU. In purely economic terms, furthermore, German hegemony relies more on suppressing labour domestically, and less on superior investment, technology, and growth performance. To remain hegemonic, Germany must continually negotiate and contest terms with other member states within EU institutions. The second factor is that German hegemony also depends on the existence of EU peripheries in a variety of ways outlined below, and is thus continually contested within the EU. The third factor is that military hegemony in the EU rests decisively with France and Britain, affording to both exceptional influence in foreign policy, although the latter country is of course due to leave the union in the coming period. German hegemony is conditional in this respect too, but military and foreign policy issues will not be considered in this book. Instead we will confine ourselves to the examination of German hegemony in the economic and political spheres.

Accounting for these aspects of EU development requires focusing on the underlying social and class relations within member states. The key factor is the opposition between capital and labour, which has clear national characteristics and never operates in a disembodied international space separate from nation states. In this respect each country of the EU, including Germany, is highly distinctive. National peculiarities have to be taken into account in analysing the neoliberal and hegemonic trajectory of the union. After all, in the capitalist world the international is always rooted in the national. However, the underlying class relations are complexly mediated among nation states, with several degrees of freedom that allow for dependence and subordination to emerge at the transnational level. Hegemony and the opposition to it are commonly observed among capitalist states. In Europe such relations are closely interwoven with the institutions of the EU and the EMU, and often hide behind a veneer of partnership.

The first analytical step that is thus required is to consider the formation of the monetary union, which has been pivotal to the neoliberal and hegemonic evolution of the EU since its inception at Maastricht.

Neoliberalism and state monopoly over money

Hayek expected a 'federal union' to be characterized by a common monetary policy and a single central bank, thus promoting 'liberalism'. In this narrow respect his expectation has certainly come true with respect to the EU. However, money is much more than a mere instrument of exchange used to facilitate trade and impose a homogenizing order on transactions. Money also embodies the asymmetric power relation between buyer and seller, while contemporary credit money further rests on the asymmetric power relation between borrower and lender.[14] The institutions and mechanisms of money are integral to power relations in the market and the economy. In this regard the euro has far transcended Hayek's expectations, casting light on the class content of neoliberalism in Europe.

Contemporary money poses a major conundrum for neoliberal ideology. Since the 1970s, neoliberal government policy has systematically promoted the deregulation of markets, while favouring the private and the individual over the social and the collective. But when it comes to the monetary sphere, the direction of neoliberal evolution has been unlike any other area of the economy. For more than four decades the final means of payment and hoarding has been fiat money issued by the state with no obligatory convertibility into anything other than itself. The public has held sway over the private.

To be sure, the prevalent form of money in most advanced countries remains private credit money created by banks and other financial institutions. However, the instrument used for final payments is money that is the monopoly of the state. Despite the relentless emphasis on competition and free markets during the last four decades, there is no competition in issuing this most important traded entity in contemporary capitalist economies. The state's monopoly over the final means of payment has indeed become absolute in the years of neoliberalism as gold has fallen completely by the wayside since the collapse of the Bretton Woods Agreement in 1971–3. A dollar is a promise by the US government to pay a dollar, and no more. This self-referential relationship rests on the authority of the state and tremendously augments its power to intervene and shape economic policy.

Neoliberalism as actual policy, rather than as ideology, has relied heavily on the state to alter the institutional structure of both economy and society in favour of markets. There is nothing 'natural' about incorporating unregulated markets in economy and society – they have to be consciously inserted.[15] Neoliberalism is a creature of the state, and has continued to lean heavily on the state throughout its ascendancy. This is at its clearest in the field of money, where the monopoly of the state has translated into exceptional power for central banks.

Central banks have emerged as the leading public economic institutions of neoliberal capitalism. Since the 1970s they have attained a position of pre-eminence that is unprecedented in the history of capitalism, and out of all proportion to the historic role of the Bank of England, the Swedish Riksbank, and other long-established central banks. By controlling the final means of payment they have been able to manage interest rates, to intervene at crucial junctures to protect the interests of the financial sector, and to confront the crises of neoliberal capitalism by providing liquidity. The ascendancy of central banks has marked the rise of neoliberalism, reflecting the pivotal role of the state.

The creation of a single currency in Europe managed by one central bank has been a decisive step in the neoliberal transformation of the EU, tilting the balance of power in favour of capital and against labour. But the euro has not been consonant with Hayek's 'liberalism', not least because it has led to the creation of a gigantic monopolist over the final means of payment across much of Europe. Indeed, Hayek, in a book published in 1976, showed himself alert to this prospect, rejecting the notion of a single currency in Europe as 'utopian' and proposing free competition in issuing money. The details of Hayek's proposal need not detain us here, and he certainly was wrong in thinking that European countries would not be 'willing to accept a common European currency'.[16] But at least he was consistent in his 'liberalism' when he argued in favour of free markets in money, rather than creating a vastly powerful monopolist of money in the European Central Bank (ECB).

The euro has propelled both neoliberalism and conditional German hegemony within the EU in ways that are partly obvious, but are also opaque and require analysis. The great historical peculiarity of the euro is that its pivotal role has been formally associated not with any single state, but with the transnational mechanisms of the EMU as a whole. This fact has critically affected the ascendancy of neoliberalism in the EU, while strongly conditioning German hegemony. It has also muddied the waters for the Left.

Creating the euro: a lever of neoliberalism and conditional German hegemony

In the late 1960s the Bretton Woods system of fixed exchange rates and controls over capital flows and other international payments began to unravel, eventually coming to an end, as was noted above, in 1971–3. The disappearance of Bretton Woods put the governments of European countries – especially smaller ones – under considerable pressure to prevent major upheavals in exchange rates and to protect their international competitiveness. It became imperative to manage payments and other obligations among European states, for which a new institutional framework was required.

The Werner Report of 1970 was the first major indication of the search for a new system.[17] The report proposed achieving a European Economic and Monetary Union in three stages, among which were included the fixing of exchange rates and the creation of a new currency. The intellectual and political debates leading to it were marked by the division between the 'economists' (i.e. mostly Germany and the Netherlands) and the 'monetarists' (i.e. mostly France and Belgium, also backed by the European Commission). The 'economist' side desired greater substantive economic convergence prior to monetary union, while the 'monetarist' side was in favour of rapid advance in creating new monetary institutions.[18] These debates already intimated future German hegemony and its conditional nature.

Broadly speaking, the 'economists' could also be thought of as 'federalists' in the sense that they advocated a gradual creation of intergovernmental institutions that would reflect greater convergence of economic practices for the union as a whole. In contrast, the 'monetarists' could be considered as 'neofunctionalists' in so far as they supported the rapid creation of new transnational institutions that would focus on exchange rate stability without requiring prior convergence of national economic practices. The analogy is helpful, though far from perfect. Germany and France led the debates and typically were on opposing sides. This division, in one form or another, has marked the entire trajectory of the EMU, certainly among the countries of the core. Nonetheless, the Werner Report led to no concrete policy or institutional outcomes – it had come before its time.

After the collapse of Bretton Woods and the turmoil that followed in the global markets in the 1970s, the pressures to manage exchange rates in Europe accumulated further. The instability caused by greatly fluctuating rates was felt particularly severely by the smaller countries of Europe. The 'Snake in the Tunnel' was adopted in 1972–3, followed for a period by the 'Snake out of the Tunnel'. The aim of these initiatives was to manage the joint fluctuations of exchange rates relative to the dollar but also relative to each other through regular interventions by central banks. The 'Tunnel' had already been created in 1971 by the Smithsonian Agreement, which followed Bretton Woods and allowed currencies to fluctuate relative to the US dollar within the margins of +2.25% and –2.25%. The 'Snake' was a further constraint imposed on EEC currencies, forcing them to move within a margin of +2.25 and –2.25% relative to each other, and thus within the 'Tunnel'. However, the 'Tunnel' came to an end in 1973 as the Smithsonian Agreement effectively failed and the dollar was allowed to fluctuate freely. The 'Snake' did not last much longer since it proved impossible to defend stable exchange rates among EEC countries as the dollar fluctuated. What began to emerge in practice in Europe was a Deutschmark area in which countries 'shadowed' the German currency and increasingly relied on it as a reserve. The seeds of German hegemony are to be found in these developments, though events after the establishment of the EMU proved far more important.

The effort to coordinate exchange rates nevertheless continued, and a decisive step was the formation of the European Monetary System (EMS) in 1979, which contained the European Exchange Rate Mechanism. Bilateral exchange rates were effectively fixed, with narrow bands on either side of par to allow for some flexibility. The key to ensuring the viability of the EMS was controlling the divergence in inflation rates among the main countries of the EMS, which meant primarily Germany, France, and Italy.[19] It also soon became clear that for the EMS to succeed it was vital to have an anchor country, which inevitably meant Germany.[20]

Any system that attempts to stabilize exchange rates without obligatory convertibility of currencies into a produced commodity, such as gold, must have an anchor country. The anchor country has to manage its domestic monetary policy, particularly its interest rates, with a view to stabilizing the exchange rate of its own currency, thus providing a firm reference point for the system as a whole. The anchor is particularly crucial when capital is able to flow relatively freely across borders, as had begun to happen in Europe in the 1980s. Free capital flows are evidently able to destabilize exchange rates, irrespective of whether the balance of trade (exports and imports) among countries is actually in balance. Moreover, if capital flows suddenly stopped, or were reversed, a foreign exchange crisis could result.

To act as anchor a country has to have sufficient economic size, measured, for instance, by its GDP; a surplus on its current account (exports, imports, income flows, and transfers); and low inflation. Germany fitted the bill perfectly for the EMS, but there was a catch: it had to manage its monetary policy by taking the entire EMS into account. If instead German monetary policy aimed at keeping domestic inflation at very low levels, the pressure of adjusting external balances would have to be shifted onto the other countries of the EMS. Specifically, if France and Italy registered inflation levels that were above the very low levels of Germany and thus began to record external deficits, they would have to accept periodic devaluations of their currencies.

The EMS worked poorly because Germany did not manage its monetary policy with a view to stabilizing exchange rates across the system. The Bundesbank, in particular, would not accept that its monetary policy should be constrained to ensure the stability of the EMS. More broadly, the German establishment aimed at manipulating the exchange rate of the Deutschmark to ensure current account surpluses. Given that Germany adopted this policy stance, tensions steadily accumulated within the EMS, particularly as France and Italy periodically had to devalue their currencies to compensate for higher inflation and loss of competitiveness relative to Germany. Depreciations were economically disruptive and politically painful for both countries.

By the early 1990s the EMS had effectively become a Deutschmark area, and the concerns of the Bundesbank had become paramount in the functioning of the system. That meant, above all, imposing inflation discipline on other countries to forestall the need for exchange rate realignments. Instead of Germany acting as the anchor of the EMS, the functioning of the system was increasingly reshaped to suit Germany and its domestic monetary policy concerns.

The EMS received a body blow in 1992 as Britain, which had only formally joined the European Exchange Rate Mechanism two years earlier, was forced to withdraw and to allow sterling to depreciate. At the time Britain had an inflation rate three times that of Germany. Attempting to keep the country in the EMS would have entailed a deep recession with major political costs. That simple fact allowed speculators to pile enormous downward pressure on sterling, continually pushing against the lower band of permitted fluctuations, and forcing the British government to spend vast sums to defend the currency. In the end Britain had to exit the system, signalling the failure of the attempt to fix the exchange rate of sterling within the EMS.

The shock of British exit from the EMS paved the way toward monetary union in the late 1990s, the landmark for which was the Delors Report in 1989.[21] The debates that led to the Delors Report, and thus eventually to the EMU, were a continuation of those between the 'economists' and the 'monetarists', except that the economic and political outlook of Europe had changed considerably during the intervening two decades. The dominant ideological approach in shaping the EMU was 'Sound Money' as advocated by the Bundesbank: that is, control over inflation broadly in line with the Quantity Theory of Money – the long-standing and deeply problematic theoretical view that the price level is driven by the supply of money.[22] Moreover, at that time economic theory across the major countries of the world economy was in thrall to arguments regarding 'time-inconsistency' in economic policy and the presumed need to create an independent central bank that would target and control inflation. These theories were important in setting the intellectual terrain for the creation of the euro.[23]

In practice, however, theoretical arguments proved secondary to determining the actual shape of the EMU. The principal role was played by the rising power of central bankers and the assertive presence of private finance in Europe already from the 1980s.[24] Thus, the EMU has had two extraordinary aspects from the beginning: first, assigning pre-eminence to monetary factors in designing the institutional structure of the euro; and, second, prescribing tough fiscal discipline on member countries. Both of these have been called the result of a 'central bankers' coup'.[25] They have certainly been at the heart of the neoliberal functioning of the monetary union.

In practice the ECB took the Bundesbank as its model and focused exclusively on maintaining a very low rate of inflation, without any obligation to finance fiscal deficits by member states. The ostensible logic was to ensure convergence of inflation rates across EMU countries, thus making it possible to stabilize international transactions in Europe and to sustain the monetary union. The actual outcome was that the operations of the common currency rebounded in the interests of German exporting capital and the EMU became a domestic market for German industry.

The political drive toward EMU, on the other hand, had quite different determinants, which again pointed to the conditional character of German hegemony. The main push came from France, true to its prominent historical role in the EU. French policy was partly a reaction to the dominant position of Germany in the EMS, but also a response to the reunification of Germany in 1990, which rekindled a host of historical concerns about German power across Europe. For the ruling social bloc of France, but also for the ruling social blocs of smaller European countries, a full monetary union seemed capable of overcoming the weaknesses of the EMS by obviating the need for an anchor country. Presumably there would be formal equality among EMU member states in reaching key monetary decisions. Moreover, the monetary union would enmesh a reunited Germany in a web of institutional practices and obligations, thus constraining its power across Europe.[26] Historical delusions rarely come grander than those of the French ruling bloc in pushing for a monetary union. The end result was to promote German hegemony conditioned by the institutions of the euro.

The nature of the emerging German hegemony can be ascertained in a further way. Broadly speaking, when the EMU was set up, the 'neo-functionalists' appeared to have won the historical argument within the EU, since a set of powerful monetary institutions were created without true convergence of economies. Moreover, by ostensibly relying on cooperation and equality, the monetary union seemed to promote greater political unity in Europe. Yet Germany ensured that the machinery of the EMU was riven by the ideology of 'Sound Money'. Furthermore, for individual countries to accede to the EMU they had to satisfy stringent criteria, which were set at Maastricht at the insistence of Germany, and will be discussed in subsequent chapters. At first sight the EMU was yet another compromise by the EU which initially appeared to favour France, but over time things turned out entirely different. The monetary union in practice favoured Germany, which learnt to navigate the straits of the common currency in the interests of its industrial exporters.

The 'architectural flaws' of the euro

It is vital at this point to consider in more detail the institutional structure of the EMU. In some fairly obvious ways the 'architecture' of the euro has been deficient from the start.[27] Mainstream economists have long been aware that the Eurozone has lacked important institutional mechanisms: for instance, a unified mechanism of fiscal transfers among states and a banking union.[28] Others have pointed to the lack of 'mutualization' of public debt – that is, allowing the debt of one member state to be considered as an obligation of another – and proposed to correct it through the issuing of Eurobonds.[29]

The fundamental institution of the EMU is the ECB, the capital for which has been contributed proportionately by all EMU member states. The ECB is part of the Eurosystem, a complex structure comprising the National Central Banks of the member countries, which have ceased to act independently with regard to designing and delivering monetary policy.[30] Nonetheless, the National Central Banks retain formal and legal responsibility over their assets and liabilities. The ECB is the pivot of the Eurosystem and is obliged by its statutes to keep inflation below 2%. It also dominates the European market for provision of liquidity among banks. The ECB does not operate under the wing of a particular state, and indeed it has historically been the most 'private' among all major central banks. Its 'private' character is evidenced by its institutional reluctance to acquire the primary debt of any state, thus desisting from the activity that typically connects a central bank to its own state in contemporary capitalism. In the course of the Eurozone crisis, however, important changes have been wrought to its practices.

The other vital institution of the EMU is the Stability and Growth Pact, which has regulated the fiscal performance of member states. The initial aim, set as the 'Maastricht Criteria', was to keep public deficits and public debt within narrow limits, respectively 3% and 60% of GDP.[31] Responsibility for enforcing the limits was left to member states. Fiscal discipline was to be bolstered by the so-called 'no bail-out clause' of the Maastricht Treaty that took a clearer form as Article 125 of the Lisbon Treaty amending Maastricht and entering into force in 2009. Article 125 basically states that the EU will not assume responsibility for the obligations and burdens of a member state.[32]

There is little doubt that the Stability and Growth Pact failed to ensure the desired fiscal discipline. There is also no doubt that Article 125 has frayed considerably at the edges in the course of the Eurozone crisis, particularly after the bail-outs of Greece, Ireland, and Portugal, and the creation of the European Stability Mechanism (ESM). Loans were certainly extended among member states to facilitate dealing with a sovereign debt crisis, thus creating a risk of non-payment. But the core provision not to share mutually in the obligations of another member state has not been directly contradicted. Furthermore, in the course of the Eurozone crisis the Pact evolved into the 'Six Pack', the 'Two Pack', the Fiscal Compact, and so on, which have hardened disciplinary controls, with sanctions available to discipline 'aberrant' states. The fiscal regime underpinning the EMU has become considerably harsher.

Compared to, say, the mechanisms of the US monetary system, the basic institutional framework of the EMU is manifestly deficient. The Federal Reserve Bank is formally able to purchase vast quantities of primary state debt, if policy necessitates it, as happened after the great crisis of 2007–9. Similarly, the US state is able to impose a uniform fiscal policy across the USA, while simultaneously ensuring the transfer of fiscal resources within the country. The ability of the USA to confront major crises is considerably greater than that of the Eurozone.

These perfectly obvious points cannot, however, provide an explanation for the travails of the EMU in the 2010s and the ensuing gigantic upheaval in Europe. Technically unexceptional as they are from an economic perspective, they are a little like blaming the clouds for producing rain. For the 'architecture' of the EMU could hardly have been different given that the monetary union was created as a treaty-based alliance among independent states that also belong to the EU. The member states of the EU have neither the legitimacy nor the desire to carry the costs and burdens of each other's actions. This is not in the least surprising among a group of sovereign states that rest on capitalist relations in their domestic economy and society.

The USA is also a sovereign state that rests on capitalist relations, but its polity and its *demos* are one. A single polity and *demos* in the EU cannot be created by diktat, and much less by stealth. The notion that there could ever be an overarching 'European' state with sufficient power to replicate the monetary practices of the US state is a figment of the bureaucratic and the academic imagination. It would take major historical events for the peoples of Europe to accept that the public debt of one country would be the direct responsibility of the government and the people of another. It is also unlikely that a permanent mechanism of fiscal transfers could be established within the EMU. Which among the nations of Europe would willingly accept the position of long-term beneficiary of another? The implications for its internal political structures, its democratic polity, its culture, and its relations with other states would be disastrous. The euro was a 'faulty' compromise, but that was inevitable among several independent nation states that created the EMU.

The broader context of conditional German hegemony

German hegemony reflects the complexity of relations among EMU and EU states. It is conditional hegemony that manifests itself through negotiating and bargaining within a complex array of institutions. It is nonetheless real and has served the interests of German big business. Indeed, given the history of state relations in Europe, the rise of Nazism, and the bloodletting of the twentieth century, that was probably the only form that German hegemony could take in the early twenty-first century.[33]

Two further aspects of the EMU have given German hegemony its peculiar, conditional form. The first is that the EMU has not simply created a common means of exchange among its members. From its inception the euro was designed to serve an international role, not only among EMU member states but also in relation to the world market. It has always been a competitor to the dollar and other global reserve currencies, a form of what Marx called 'world money'.[34]

World money is qualitatively different from national monies because it acts as a means of payment and a means of hoarding in the world market, a role that gold has historically played for centuries, and which has been assumed by the US dollar for decades. Control over world money is a lever of power at the global level, a means of hegemony on a par with military power. The euro is a peculiar form of world money because it has been created *ex nihilo* through the monetary union of several states of vastly different economic and political power. There is nothing 'natural' or 'spontaneous' about the emergence of the euro in the contemporary international markets, and that is a source of both strength and weakness.

To act as a world reserve currency the euro has had to gain global acceptability and credibility from scratch, and its institutional mechanisms were designed partly with this purpose in mind. The ECB and the Eurosystem were created with the express aim of ensuring price stability, which is necessary for the euro to act as a reserve of value. The global acceptability of the euro, on the other hand, encouraged the imposition of fiscal rigidity among member states, including the Growth and Stability Pact.

The second aspect determining Germany's conditional hegemony is that the euro was created in a period of rapid financialization of advanced economies, including leading countries such as Germany and France, and peripheral countries such as Portugal and Greece. Financialization signifies the ascendancy of the private financial sector relative to the rest of the economy, and has characterized the development of capitalism during the last four decades.[35] The non-financial sector in mature countries has performed comparatively poorly, marked by weak corporate investment and low productivity growth. Furthermore, there has been a growing involvement of households and individuals with the private financial sector to borrow for housing and consumption, but also to manage pensions, insurance, and other assets.

The EMU has served the interests of large European multinationals and financial institutions under conditions of advancing financialization. Price stability and control over inflation is a *sine qua non* for lenders and for financial capital. A homogeneous internal market for borrowing supported by liquidity generated by a powerful central bank was necessary for European banks to spread their operations globally. Fiscal discipline is typically required by lenders and by banks alike to protect their loan advances. To gain competitive advantages in the world market, industrial capital requires labour 'flexibility', and the euro has been an outstanding instrument for imposing discipline on workers, particularly in the years of crisis. In short, financialization in Europe received a boost through the introduction of the euro, although significant differences exist in this respect among core countries as well as between the core and the periphery.

Nearly three decades after Maastricht, the conditional hegemony of Germany in the EU is undeniable, as is the role played by the euro in ensuring it. There was no German plan to achieve such an outcome when the euro was first mooted. Nonetheless, Germany came to dominate the union as neoliberalism gained sway across the EU. Banking and industrial capitals have drawn considerable benefits while the costs have been borne by working people, not least in Germany. Conditions of exceptional instability have been created in both economy and society across Europe, climaxing in the Eurozone crisis, with disastrous implications for countries and social classes. By this token the existence of German hegemony remains under threat. These issues are considered in the rest of this book.

3

The Ascendancy of Germany and the Division of Europe

A distinctive financialized economy

Germany is the dominant economy and the hegemonic country of the EU.[1] It has a large and globally competitive industrial base, pivoting on automobiles, chemicals, and machine tools. Its exports allow it to command vast surpluses on its current account, thus providing it with the wherewithal to lend globally. Export surpluses and international lending based on industrial strength are the foundation of German hegemony in Europe. The contrast with France, whose industry has proportionately declined, is sharp. Among EU countries only Italy has an industrial base that could allow it potentially to compete on broadly comparable terms with Germany.

The success of Germany, however, is not due to a wave of investment, or technological progress and productivity improvements in recent decades. Indeed, the performance of the country in these fields is unremarkable. Germany's current ascendancy is not comparable to its previous rise at the end of the nineteenth century, despite also being based on heavy industry. Contemporary Germany is marked by a particular variant of financialized capitalism, which has allowed it to dominate the EU but nonetheless produced a historically mediocre economic performance. German capitalism appears successful because other mature countries in Europe – and the USA – have performed poorly in the decades of financialization.

The peculiarities of financialized capitalism in Germany stand in contrast to financialization in the USA and Britain, and also in France.[2] First, and similarly to other financialized countries, the German non-financial corporate sector has been reluctant to invest its profits, thereby accumulating tremendous volumes of liquid resources available for financial transactions and lending. During the last four decades the German service sector has become proportionately larger, as should be expected from a financialized economy, but the country has also systematically defended its industrial sector, not least by manipulating the exchange rate to protect exports. The distinctive feature of German financialization is the maintenance of a strong industrial base in spite of weak aggregate investment.[3]

Of particular importance in this respect is that the German manufacturing sector is highly productive, export-oriented, and has maintained relatively strong union representation in the wage formation process compared to the rest of the private sector, which has modest productivity and relatively weak unions. Wage coordination tends to be stronger in German manufacturing than in other EU countries.[4] These distinctive aspects of the German economy, including its wage bargaining structures, have proved crucial to the export-based ascendancy of Germany since the late 1990s.

Second, the German financial system has retained much of its historic character as 'bank-based', in contrast to the 'market-based' finance in Anglo-Saxon countries. Germany continues to assign a stronger role to banks compared to the stock market, a feature that has important implications for the governance of large corporations as well as for the relationship between corporations, banks, and the state. Specifically, long-term relations are easier to develop among corporations and banks, and the internal structure of corporations is not driven by the requirement to placate stock markets on a constant basis. Greater scope is also created for state intervention in the relations between labour and capital.

Not least in this regard is the distinction between large German banks that operate globally and a raft of small and medium banks, the *Sparkassen*, that operate with a local focus. Also important are public banks that continue to play a significant role in the German system, including a long-term investment bank, the KfW. German banks have followed the general trends of financialization, shifting their focus away from financing corporate investment and aiming to make profits out of financial transactions and dealing with households. But the differences with Anglo-Saxon countries remain profound.

Third, German financialization vividly differs from Anglo-Saxon and also from French financialization with regard to households and individuals. German household debt is proportionately lower and has actually declined relative to GDP for several years. Crucial in this respect is that the German system of housing provision does not favour mortgage finance, a feature that has restrained household indebtedness. Similarly, the mobilization of private savings to make funds available for stock market transactions is not comparable to the USA and Britain. The financialization of everyday life is present in Germany, but not nearly to the same degree as in the Anglo-Saxon countries, or France.[5]

Preparing for the EMU and adopting the euro in the 1990s facilitated German financialization, as is clear with regard to relations between labour and capital. Generally speaking, financialization is associated with downward pressure on real wages, rising inequality, and worsening conditions of labour, and Germany has been among the global leaders in these respects. Stagnation of wages, rising inequality, and burgeoning growth of precarious labour have marked the adoption of the euro in Germany, as is shown in further detail below. Downward pressure on wages has been general across the economy and notable in manufacturing.[6] This is the true source of German hegemony in the EU, and simultaneously its greatest weakness.

The suppression of German labour was further conditioned by a series of other developments that have subjected German workers to ever more powerful pressures. Crucial in this respect has been German reunification in 1990, which devastated the East German economy by exposing the region's enterprises to West German costs and prices, a process rendered all the more excruciating by the government's decision to swap the East German mark at the rate of one to one for the West German Deutschmark. A great mass of unemployed – and unemployable – labour was thereby created in the

East, which has exerted continuous downward pressure on wages in the West.

The collapse of the Eastern Bloc detonated a further transformation in the long run. The opening of Poland, Hungary, the Czech Republic, Slovakia, and Slovenia, with their relatively high-skilled and low-cost labour, presented German manufacturing capital with a wonderful opportunity.[7] International supply chains have become a vital feature of financialized capitalism, allowing manufacturers to shift some parts of production to cheaper locations abroad while often finishing output at home, and thus generating great volumes of trade within the same sector. Since the early 1990s German enterprises have engaged in building manufacturing supply chains in Europe (and elsewhere) by relocating productive capacity partly to other core countries, including the Netherlands and Austria, and partly to countries of the former Eastern Bloc. By taking advantage of the low wages, well-trained labour force, and institutional capacities of the former Eastern Bloc countries, they have turned these into a periphery for German capital, while adding wage pressure on workers in German labour markets.

In sum the ascendancy of financialized Germany in the EU has its roots in changes in the German domestic class balance between capital and labour. German capital has prevailed over German labour for several decades. On this basis it has come to dominate the EU, but it also induced the gigantic Eurozone crisis in 2010–12. German hegemony proved crucial in the subsequent restructuring of the EMU. It is necessary, therefore, to consider more closely the defeat of German labour.

The defeat of German labour in the 1990s

The run-up to the EMU in the 1990s was marked by a substantial weakening of the place of labour in the German economy.[8] In the preceding years German capitalists had already begun a process of seceding from their union contracts, union density had fallen significantly, and non-union labour had expanded.[9] Concern within government circles about persistent high unemployment was exacerbated by the approach of the common currency. Meanwhile, neoliberal economics dominated German policy-making circles, giving credence to the notion that wage restraint is the key to increasing employment. The Social Democratic government of Gerhard Schröder in the late 1990s and early 2000s seized upon the already weakened state of labour and the ideological dominance of neoliberalism to consolidate the subordination of the working class by German employers.

Neoliberalism in Germany was promoted by Anglo-Saxon-trained economists, who have come to dominate the major universities during the last several decades. Neoliberal policies also have German roots in 'ordo-liberalism', an ideological mix that is in favour of the virtues of the market while advocating strong state intervention to ensure economic freedom and protect social cohesion. The German establishment has always been highly suspicious of post-war Keynesian economics.[10] However, ordoliberalism is not about social paternalism, and nor does it advocate a practical compromise between capital and labour by offering protection to the latter. At its core lies the rule of law as the principle that consciously regulates competition and motivates

45

government intervention to avoid pernicious outcomes created by the market. It is an approach to the market that is rooted in legal theory and seeks order through integral coordination of competition by the state.

It is important to stress that the by-passing of democracy in the EU, and even more the policies to defend the EMU, have run counter to ordoliberal notions. The EU has turned the operation of the single market into a technocratic realm, a constellation of rules, which have at times required emergency measures on the part of the state. In particular, rescuing the EMU in the 2010s has relied on a raft of emergency measures of non-existent or dubious legality, as is shown below in the context of Greece. These practices were directly against the spirit and the letter of German ordoliberalism. In practice, ordoliberalism has been in retreat in Germany in the face of rising Anglo-Saxon neoliberalism that does not rely on the legal grounding of the market to motivate government intervention.[11] Last but not least in this respect the path of German society since the adoption of the euro has been marked by anything but greater social cohesion.

During the last two decades and more, class differences have been sharply exacerbated in Germany, inequality has increased, and precarious employment has swept across the labour force.[12] The Schröder government's so-called 'Agenda 2010' promoted deregulation of the labour market, giving enterprises greater freedom to hire and fire. At the same time rules were loosened to permit the increase of part-time and temporary jobs, leading to an extraordinary rise of precarious employment. Even more consequential was the introduction of the so-called 'Hartz Reforms', particularly those referring to unemployment benefits (Hartz IV). A guaranteed minimum living allowance was introduced, but the unemployed were also forced to seek and take work that hitherto might not have been considered. The protection of German workers in the labour market was profoundly weakened and wage pressures intensified.[13]

The overall outcome of the Hartz Reforms was to render German workers much more subject to the demands of their employers, undercutting their ability to resist. However, the importance of the changes that occurred in the late 1990s and early 2000s was to be found less in their specific effects of wages and work practices and more in the undisguised expulsion of labour from its traditional place in the corporatist structure of the German economy. This was no gradual reform that was mutually accepted by capital, labour, and the state. It represented a sudden shock delivered from above, which had the explicit effect of demoting the German working class as a political player. The institutional practices that had shaped the trajectory of German capitalism in the post-war years, ensuring a triangular bargaining relationship between employers' associations, trade unions, and the state, received a body blow. In particular, wage moderation was accepted in the relatively highly unionized manufacturing sector, while in the service sector, which has much weaker unions, or even no unions at all across large parts of it, wage moderation was not effectively resisted. In the public sector, moreover, the application of fiscal austerity, which meant downward pressure on wages, became institutionalized from the mid-1990s and was often ahead of wage moderation in the private sector.[14]

The implications of this signal defeat of the German

working class for the evolution of the EMU were dramatic. German nominal wages were prevented from rising virtually at all from the end of the 1990s to the end of the 2000s, as is shown in the following section. The result was that, on the one hand, inflation was systematically kept low and, on the other, the distribution of income was equally systematically shifted in favour of capital. The gains of productivity, such as they were during this period, accrued to capital. For German society as a whole the consequences were equally severe. The social democratic spirit that marked the distribution of income – prevalent in the Federal Republic during the first post-war decades – finally evaporated. United Germany became a harshly unequal society in which the functional distribution of income continued to move relentlessly in favour of capital, as it had been doing already since the 1980s.[15] The income share of labour collapsed.

Meanwhile, for the competitors of Germany inside the Eurozone the outcome was a fall in their competitiveness, as long as they were unable to match Germany's wage restraint and low inflation. Put differently, the German real effective exchange rate declined systematically, since low nominal wage increases are closely correlated with low inflation. Membership of the EMU meant that the loss of competitiveness by other countries could not be countermanded by the long-standing device of lowering exchange rates: that is, by devaluing to reduce costs and prices. The fundamental conditions for triggering the Eurozone crisis were put in place.

The implications of this defeat for labour for the broader functioning of German economy were also far-reaching. The suppression of wage growth that made for Germany's export success also ensured weak growth of domestic consumption. Aggregate demand was pushed downward, thus lowering the growth of domestic German GDP. The weakness of consumption was far from counteracted by a rise in investment since the most striking aspect of the German economy during the last two decades has been the failure to expand investment in new plant and equipment, paralleled by weak public investment in infrastructure. The consequence has been weak productivity growth for the economy as a whole.

In sum, Germany's rising competitiveness and export growth since the late 1990s has been based less on its ability to raise output per person and more on its capacity to suppress compensation per person. Germany has witnessed strong external dynamism but a cramped pattern of internal expansion. A sharp distinction has emerged between the export sector of the economy, which is highly productive and competitive, and the domestic sector, which is considerably weaker. The tremendous pressures exercised by German employers on German workers have led to the country's contradictory development within the EMU, examined in more detail in the following section.

The competitive advantage of Germany and the creation of the Southern periphery

As was shown in the previous chapter, the EMU placed monetary policy in the hands of the ECB and fiscal policy in the straitjacket of the Stability and Growth Pact. Inevitably the pressure of adjustment in economic relations among Eurozone members fell on the labour market. The results were eventually inimical to wage labour across Europe, and the main victor of the ensuing intensification of class conflict was German industrial capital.

The proximate cause of the Eurozone crisis was a violent reversal of capital flows into the crisis countries owing to large deficits on their current accounts and large volumes of public debt – a 'sudden stop'. To account fully for the Eurozone 'sudden stop' of the 2010s, however, it is imperative to start with German domestic policies. Its roots lie with capital–labour relations in Germany.

It is striking in this respect that the official machinery of the EU has largely evaded the issue of German domestic labour policies when faced with the crisis, partly because it was unwilling to confront Germany directly. The preferred approach of the European Commission has been to attribute much of the blame for the crisis to a loss of competitiveness among peripheral countries.[16] Presumably, competitiveness was lost for reasons internal to the countries hit by the crisis, including institutional weaknesses and various market inefficiencies, above all, in the labour markets. The conclusion naturally followed that a remedial policy of 'reforms' was necessary to confront the crisis, and the test case and field of application of these policies was Greece.

The Commission paid much less attention to another aspect of national competitiveness within the EMU, namely divergences in nominal unit labour costs. National competitiveness is a notoriously difficult concept to define, and it is certainly not the same as enterprise competitiveness, which depends on technology, labour skills, quality of management, and other similar factors.[17] National competitiveness, other things being equal, depends on the rate of domestic inflation (negatively) and on the rate of aggregate productivity change (positively). For this reason, a good proxy for its evolution is the rate of change of nominal unit labour cost.

In somewhat more technical terms, nominal unit labour cost is defined as the ratio of the nominal remuneration of labour divided by the economy's real output. The nominal remuneration of labour includes not only nominal wages but also all other nominal labour costs for employers. The real output of a national economy, on the other hand, is defined as nominal output divided by the price level. Empirically, the rate of change of nominal unit labour cost over time is closely correlated with inflation.[18] Moreover, if both the numerator and the denominator of the ratio were divided by the total hours worked in the economy, the numerator would then stand for the nominal cost of labour per hour worked, while the denominator would stand for labour productivity. Therefore, the path of nominal unit labour cost over time would also reflect the variation of nominal labour remuneration relative to labour productivity.

Figure 1 shows the trajectory of nominal unit labour costs since the actual introduction of the euro in 1999 for France, Germany, Greece, Italy, and Spain. This mix of countries was chosen to represent the core and the Southern periphery of the EU. Italy is a country with a foot in both camps, not least owing to the sustained weakness of the economy in its own south.

The path of each country is shown in relation to

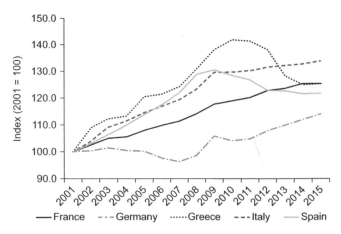

Figure 1 Nominal unit labour costs
Source: Constructed from AMECO data.

itself, with 2001 equal to 100. The gap between any two curves represents loss of national competitiveness for the country with the faster rising costs. Note that the curves show changes rather than levels of competitiveness, since what matters ultimately for trade imbalances are divergences of competitiveness, rather than absolute levels. The change in competitiveness shown in Figure 1 is cumulative over the period.

The country that stands out – the true outlier in the EMU – is Germany. Nominal unit labour costs essentially froze in Germany for more than a decade as a result of the dramatic shift in the balance of power in favour of capital and against labour. Germany made enormous gains in national competitiveness in the 2000s, which had nothing to do with improving labour productivity. Indeed, the performance of the aggregate German economy with regard to productivity has been worse than Greece, as is shown in Figure 2.[19] There

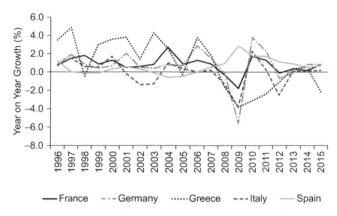

Figure 2 Real labour productivity per person
Source: Constructed from AMECO data.

has been no German 'productivity miracle' in the last two decades. The core industrial sectors of the German economy remain highly productive, particularly export-oriented manufacturing, but for the economy as a whole productivity gains have been poor.

The foundation of the tremendous trading success of Germany since the introduction of the euro has been extraordinary domestic wage restraint – German exports have boomed on the back of German workers. German exporting industries exploited the monetary union as well as the changes wrought by reunification in the 1990s to gain an advantage over labour, thus paving the way for the country's international ascendancy. The domestic conditions of German labour, on the other hand, have worsened in line with the victory of capital.

The broader impact of the tremendous competitiveness gains made by Germany was decisive. Within the monetary union there was no way that other countries

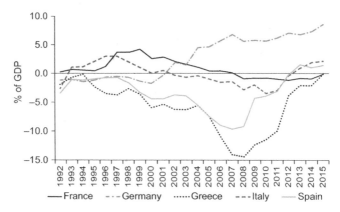

Figure 3 Current account as percentage of GDP
Source: Constructed from AMECO data.

could adjust their exchange rates to eliminate the German gains. A pronounced transformation began to take place in the trading patterns of the member states of the EMU, shifting from fairly constrained variations until the late 1990s, to a huge surplus for Germany matched by deficits for others, as is shown in Figure 3. In the 2000s the jump in the external surplus of Germany derived mostly from within the Eurozone. However, in the 2010s German exports have also been successful in broader markets, though for reasons still associated with the euro, as is discussed below.

The creation of the EMU allowed Germany to implement a neo-mercantilist policy of keeping domestic demand weak by suppressing wages, while seeking growth by ensuring external surpluses. Through its surpluses the country sucked in demand from across Europe in the 2000s, and has done so from across the world in the 2010s. The mirror image of Germany's exporting triumph has been the emergence of a Southern Eurozone periphery that has faced enormous deficits on its current account. German neo-mercantilism has also placed France and Italy in an impossible predicament, facing persistent pressures on their current accounts and difficulty to compete internationally.

For the countries of the periphery the most pressing aspect of the growing external imbalances in the 2000s was the rise in indebtedness, induced by the need to finance the deficits. The form taken by debt varied among peripheral countries depending crucially on the domestic array of economic and political factors. It is beyond dispute, however, that the main increase took place in private debt.[20] Figure 4 shows the trajectory of debt incurred by non-financial agents in the economy, that is, by corporations and households. It is important to note that the debt incurred by financial

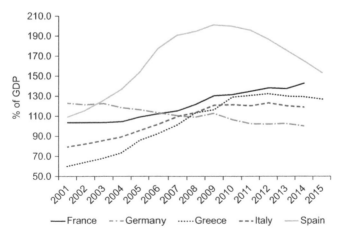

Figure 4 Private debt (non-financial corporations and households) as percentage of GDP

Source: Constructed from AMECO data.

agents – that is, primarily by banks – was generally even more substantial, but is not shown in the figure for simplicity. In the 2000s there was a veritable explosion of Spanish private debt – a direct result of the real estate bubble that occurred following accession to the EMU – and there was also a substantial increase in Greece, although there was no real estate bubble.

In sharp contrast to private debt, public debt as a proportion of GDP generally declined or was stable for most of the 2000s, as is shown in Figure 5. Public debt did not cause the Eurozone crisis, even in Greece. The rapid increase in public debt in Europe took place after the outbreak of the crisis.

The accumulation of debt by the Southern periphery occurred primarily owing to the periphery's loss of competitiveness and the attendant external deficits. To be sure, foreign banks lent to peripheral countries, for instance to the Greek state and to Spanish private

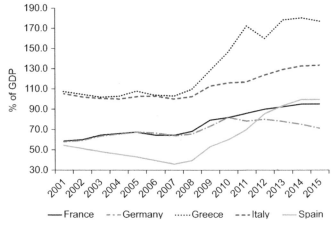

Figure 5 Public debt as percentage of GDP
Source: Constructed from AMECO data.

banks. Peripheral borrowing, however, was a reflection of the underlying inability of these economies to compete, which meant that they had to finance their external deficits through foreign flows of money capital. The accumulation of debt abroad was a macroeconomic result of declining competitiveness.

The accumulation of private debt in the Eurozone, furthermore, resulted from the strong growth of domestic finance in member countries reflecting the boost given to financialization by the euro. A common monetary policy and a homogeneous interbank market across the Eurozone forced nominal long-term interest rates to converge toward the same low level in Europe in the 2000s. Nominal interest rates in the Southern periphery dropped to unprecedentedly low levels, as is shown in Figure 6. Lower nominal and real rates in the periphery coupled with the heightened ability of peripheral banks to obtain liquidity in the interbank markets of the EMU led to a tremendous growth of domestic finance. For the Southern periphery the 2000s were a period of financial

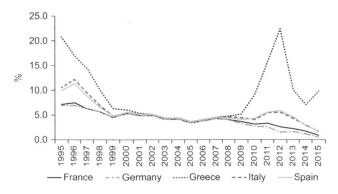

Figure 6 Nominal long-term interest rates
Source: Constructed from AMECO data.

expansion as households and workers were brought into the realm of formal finance to obtain real estate and consumption loans.

The counterpart to rising peripheral debt was the emergence of Germany as a major lender, both in Europe and across the world. Figure 7 shows the historic jump in the trade and current account surpluses of Germany following the introduction of the euro, which have amounted to a vast improvement in the country's net international investment position.[21]

To sum up, following the introduction of the EMU, Germany emerged as a major industrial exporter and a major lender across Europe and the world, by drawing primarily on the weakness of its domestic labour. In so doing, Germany set the ground for the out-

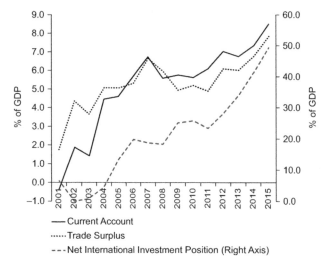

Figure 7 German balance of payments statistics as percentage of GDP

Source: Constructed from AMECO data.

break of the Eurozone crisis in 2010 as well as for the division of the EMU into a core and a Southern periphery.

The unstable core of the EMU and the Central European periphery

German ascendancy has generated considerable weakness in the core of the EMU as France and Italy have been unable to compete against Germany.[22] But it has also led to the emergence of a Central European periphery comprising Poland, the Czech Republic, Hungary, Slovakia, and Slovenia, which is quite distinct from the Southern periphery, not least since much of it lies outside the EMU. These divisions within the EU are of critical importance and will shape the future development of Europe.[23] At the very least they indicate that there will be no convergence of economies within the EU. Strongly fissiparous economic tendencies have emerged which underpin the disintegrating tendencies of the EU at the level of society and politics.

Figure 8 shows the trajectory of the current account of the core shown separately for Germany compared to the other two countries as well as for the Southern and the Central European periphery. The historic upward shift in the German current account surplus is apparent, and is mostly due to the export of industrially produced commodities. After the outbreak of the Eurozone crisis, which constrained markets within the Eurozone, the German surplus began to derive increasingly from trade with the rest of the world. German industries took advantage of the weakness of the euro, and Germany

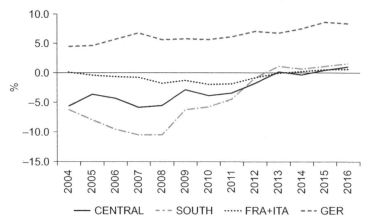

Figure 8 Current account of core and peripheries as percentage of GDP

Source: Constructed from AMECO data.

came to dominate the internal market of the EMU, while also benefiting globally.

The contrast with France and Italy is pronounced. Taken together they registered deficits on their current accounts in the 2000s, and have swung to a small surplus in the 2010s. The source of the surplus in recent years was Italy, which has consistently applied austerity measures that have depressed domestic demand, and thus imports. France continued to register deficits, since it did not apply austerity policies to a significant extent during this period. Germany ascendancy has rent asunder the core of the Eurozone, turning Italy into the weakest link.

The contrast between Germany and the two peripheries is similarly pronounced, but so is the contrast between the two peripheries. The Southern periphery registered large deficits in the 2000s, which were the immediate cause of the Eurozone crisis. The deficits have turned into small surpluses in the 2010s as austerity and bail-out programmes have been imposed by the EU. In contrast, the Central European periphery registered small deficits in the 2000s and has witnessed small surpluses in the 2010s. The external trading relations of the two peripheries have followed very different trajectories reflecting the different evolution of their economies.

Figure 9 brings out the fissiparous tendencies by showing the trajectory of industrial output for these groups of countries. The strong performance of German industry and the corresponding decline of France and Italy are clear. Even more striking, however, is the contrast between the two peripheries. The Southern periphery comprises economies with a weakening industrial base. They also have a large service sector and have historically relied on a sizeable public sector to act as

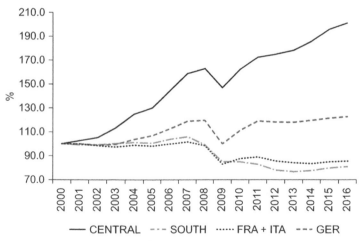

Figure 9 Industrial production (excluding construction, 2000 = 100)

Source: Constructed from AMECO data.

a mass employer. In contrast, the Central European periphery comprises economies that have a strengthening industrial base. They also have a relatively weaker service sector and their public sector does not act as a mass employer.

Several domestic factors have dictated the ascent of industry in the Central European periphery compared to the South, including a well-trained and relatively compliant labour force. The two following elements, however, stand out.

First, there has been a sustained expansion of German industrial capital in Central Europe in the form of foreign direct investment (FDI), acquiring productive capacity and integrating these economies into the German industrial base. The focus of German FDI has been in manufacturing, especially in automobiles, and has resulted in a high proportion of 'greenfield' investments. Extensive supply chains have been created which often export parts of the manufacturing process to peripheral countries, while producing the finished output in Germany, thus lowering costs. The result has been considerable growth of intra-industry trade, which has further boosted industrial capacity in Central Europe by providing opportunities to large numbers of local small-scale suppliers. Second, Poland, the Czech Republic, and Hungary, which are the leading countries of the Central European periphery and the main recipients of German FDI, are not members of the EMU. They have avoided the competitiveness trap and the austerity vice of the EMU that has throttled the South. When necessary, they have been able to rely on exchange rate policy.

To pursue these points further consider the alloca-

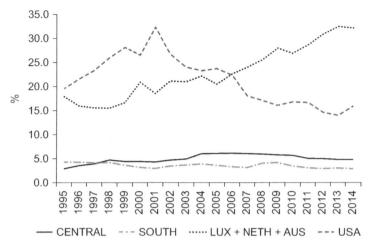

Figure 10 German outward FDI as percentage of total
Source: Constructed from Bundesbank data.

tion of German outward FDI. Figure 10 shows that there have been pronounced changes in the allocation of German outward FDI roughly since the time of the introduction of the euro. First, the share allocated to the USA, which used to be by far the largest recipient, has declined precipitously, while those allocated to the three core countries of the EMU, namely the Netherlands, Luxembourg, and Austria, have risen equally sharply.[24] Second, the proportion of German FDI that has gone to the Central European periphery has been a relatively small part of the whole. Third, the proportion of German FDI going to the Southern periphery is insignificant and declining.

It is clear that the emergence of the EMU was a landmark for German industrial capital, encouraging it to expand in a broad geographical area contiguous to its national territory.[25] The great bulk of FDI is still primarily directed to other core areas of the EU rather than seeking to move to the periphery. However, German supply chains have also expanded significantly in Central Europe, even if German FDI in the region has been proportionately declining for more than a decade. The contrast with the South is striking.

The Central European periphery has been partially integrated into the German industrial complex, with corresponding patterns of trade. The availability of cheap Central European labour has allowed Germany to maintain downward pressure on wages at home, even if unemployment has been falling in Central Europe in recent years and wages have edged upward. At the same time, Central European periphery economies have come to depend heavily on Germany for technology and markets. If Germany faced a serious recession, so would probably the whole of Central Europe. Southern Europe, in contrast, is far less integrated into the German industrial base, as is reflected in its trade patterns. Southern economies rely heavily on services, including tourism, and their technological level is generally weak. Nonetheless, both peripheries have been exporting skilled labour to Germany, thus weakening their potential for productivity increases.

Finally, lest it be thought that German ascendancy in the EU has resulted in the resurgence of the continent as a whole as a productive force in the world economy, consider Figure 11, which shows domestic investment as a proportion of GDP. German aggregate investment has been notably weak as German industrial capital has tended to turn its enormous profits into monetary surpluses that are hoarded or invested abroad. Investment in France and Italy has also been consist-

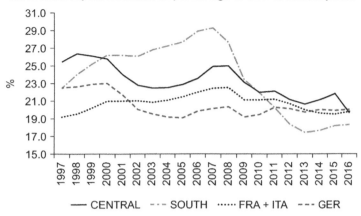

Gross fixed capital formation as percentage of GDP at current prices

Figure 11 Investment in core and peripheries as percentage of GDP

Source: Constructed from AMECO data.

ently weak, particularly in the aftermath of the great crisis of 2007–9 and the Eurozone crisis. Investment in the Southern periphery has completely collapsed, but note that investment in the Central European periphery has also been weak and declining. German ascendancy is not based on any kind of 'miracle' in Germany, and nor has it resulted in broad-based conditions of prosperity in the EU and the EMU. Rather, it is premised on relentless pressure on German workers within the framework of the EMU, and its foundations are correspondingly precarious.

This is the underlying economic and social reality that will shape the path of the EU in the years to come. There can be little doubt that the EMU has been a historical failure in terms of promoting stability and convergence in Europe. Its historic role has been to help German industrial capital establish its supremacy across the continent. In determining its attitude toward the EU, the Left in Europe must depart from these material realities rather than from abstract generalities about European unity, shared prosperity, and so on. To this purpose it is vital to consider closely the Eurozone crisis and particularly the responses to it by the institutions and governments of Europe.

4

The Eurozone Crisis:
Class Interests and
Hegemonic Power

The crisis erupts

At the end of the 2000s the Southern periphery of the EMU found itself in an extremely precarious position marked by huge external deficits and accumulated debt, as was shown in Figures 3, 4, and 5. The spark that lit the fire was the global crisis of financialization in 2007–9, which began in the USA and led to a banking collapse in 2008, the contraction of credit, and a synchronized recession across the world in 2008–9.[1] Governments intervened to buttress the financial sector by injecting capital and providing liquidity, while also shoring up economic activity by supporting aggregate demand. By late 2009 the worst of the global crisis was over as global banking began to stabilize, and developing countries in particular returned to growth. But the recession and government intervention meant that large fiscal deficits had emerged and public debt had begun to accelerate. For the Southern periphery these developments were catastrophic since they ignited the Eurozone crisis in 2010.[2]

In narrow economic terms the Eurozone turmoil was a balance of payments crisis involving a sudden reversal of capital flows from abroad. This phenomenon has occurred frequently in developing countries in the decades since the 1980s, often taking the form of a 'sudden stop' crisis.[3] Characteristic of such crises is that private international lenders (banks, other large financial institutions, etc.) stop lending to governments and even to private borrowers of countries that register combinations of large external deficits, fiscal deficits, and debts. The lenders seek instead to ensure repayment of loans already made and to protect themselves. Liquidity consequently becomes scarce in financial markets. A country that finds itself in the eye of the storm typically faces difficulties even borrowing to meet immediate obligations, particularly to service its accumulated external debt. Often the prospect of default arises, leading to a tremendous escalation of pressure.

A country faced with an acute 'sudden stop' has to secure fresh liquidity and funds to allow its government and private economic agents to continue to meet immediate obligations. But the international financial system lacks formal mechanisms with which to tackle this task. In recent decades that role has devolved on multilateral organizations, such as the International Monetary Fund (IMF), the central banks of powerful states, and the governments of states that register large surpluses on their external transactions. The IMF has accumulated much experience in coordinating policy responses typically aimed at developing countries. Funds and liquidity are provided in the form of loans invariably with 'conditionality' attached, that is, with a harsh set of demands imposed on the borrower. 'Conditionality' reflects power relations among the states that borrow and those that lend, but also projects and defends class interests in both borrowing and lending countries. Not least, over the years 'conditionality' has helped impose a neoliberal policy agenda on stricken countries.

The Eurozone 'sudden stop' crisis resulted from the profound imbalances that had built up in the EMU in the 2000s. By late 2009 is was clear that the huge volumes of public debt in Greece, but also of private debt in Spain and elsewhere, would be impossible to sustain through regular access to the international markets. In early 2010 private lenders (typically German and French) took fright and began sharply to reverse the flow of loanable capital to the Southern periphery, seeking instead to have their older loans paid off. In particular, private bank lending by the core to the periphery of the Eurozone essentially dried up.[4]

The 'stop' forced Greece, followed by Portugal and Ireland, out of financial markets in 2010, making it impossible to borrow and service public debt. But the Eurozone crisis was not a common 'sudden stop' crisis similar to those in developing countries in previous decades. If it were, a foreign exchange crisis would have materialized and exchange rates would have fallen sharply once the private capital flows had collapsed. The fall in the exchange rate would have exacerbated the financial pressures by making loans from abroad even riskier, but it would also have attenuated the ensuing recession by boosting exports and reducing imports. Unfortunately for the countries of the Southern periphery their possession of a common currency, the euro, meant that there were no foreign exchange rates that could fall. The Eurozone 'sudden stop' crisis acquired a peculiar and sinister form, forcing the economies and societies of the Southern periphery to take the full impact of the shock. The implications proved dramatic for workers and the poor as well as for interstate relations.

Imposing a neoliberal agenda

The response of the EU to the shock of 2010 transformed a crisis of capital flows, international trade, and external debt into an economic and social disaster for the periphery, especially in Greece. It affirmed the hold of neoliberalism across the EMU while also revealing the sharp side of German hegemony. EU policy defended primarily the interests of big business, and especially banks, at the expense of wage labour and the poor. Perhaps worst of all, it did not fully resolve the crisis but rather pacified it, and has left the EMU in a still precarious position at the end of the 2010s.

The paramount concern of the EU was to prevent the monetary union from collapsing, and to defend the euro as an international reserve currency. To this purpose it was imperative to protect the interests of banks, particularly those of the core. It was also necessary to boost the regime of fiscal discipline that was already integral to the monetary union. For the EU, the monetary union had to continue functioning in accordance with Maastricht, which meant that the existing framework had to be made stronger and harsher. The costs would be borne by the countries directly hit by the crisis as well as by working people across the EU.

To be more specific, EU policy was based on the view that the crisis was caused by a loss of competitiveness by peripheral countries owing to their putative institutional weaknesses. These included, presumably: inadequate fiscal controls on government; weak taxation systems; collective bargaining and protection for workers against firing; extensive public ownership of productive and other resources; generous pension systems; restrictive regulations in goods and services markets; bank loans advanced on concessional and even corrupt terms; and so on.

On these grounds the Commission imposed a host of neoliberal policies on the stricken Southern periphery, most notably fiscal austerity and wage reductions, along with deregulation and privatization. These neoliberal policies were supposed to achieve 'stabilization' by compressing domestic demand, thus reducing imports and the deficit on the current account. At the same time they were supposed to improve competitiveness and increase exports, thus stimulating growth. The measures were designed and overseen by the notorious Troika, that is, the Commission, the ECB, and the IMF, with the IMF's technical expertise providing theoretical and empirical backing. The ECB in particular demanded immediate implementation of neoliberal measures even from the governments of large countries, such as Spain and Italy. Its arrogant and domineering tone left little doubt regarding the balance of power within the EU in the early 2010s.[5]

From the point of view of the functioning of the EU the most striking aspect of the Troika was that it was unelected and largely unaccountable. There was to be no democracy in dealing with the crisis; indeed democracy would be deliberately side-lined, most egregiously in Greece. Moreover, a host of other unelected, informal, and unaccountable mechanisms of the EU acquired tremendous power during the crisis, including the Eurogroup and the Eurogroup Working Group. These bodies, comprising professional politicians and economic experts, took decisions that affected the lives of tens of millions across Europe. A clearer instance of the hollowing-out of democracy in the EU is hard to imagine.

Broadly speaking, EU policies were of a piece with the neoliberal approach to developing country crises adopted by the IMF since the early 1980s, which gradually came to constitute the 'Washington Consensus' in economic policy. This is a neoliberal totem that has become characteristic of financialized capitalism and broadly advocates financial and labour market deregulation, fiscal austerity, and privatization. Over the years the 'Washington Consensus' has given rise to an extensive critical literature owing to its theoretical weaknesses and policy blunders.[6] Far from curing the problems of stricken economies, austerity frequently has had a net destructive effect on output, employment, and productive capacity. Similarly, there is little evidence that privatization and deregulation induce rapid growth. The ruinous aspects of these policies will be considered in the next chapter in relation to Greece.

In addition to fiscal austerity, deregulation, and privatization, the EU response to the crisis also involved shifting great volumes of private debt onto the ledger of the public sector, especially in Spain and Ireland. Instead of Spanish and Irish banks declaring default and taking losses for their shareholders and bondholders, their debts were assumed by the public through the government. Shifting private debt onto the public sector of peripheral countries protected the lending banks of the core, especially in Germany and France. For, if peripheral banks had declared bankruptcy, core banks would have found themselves in deep trouble. The costs of the crisis were thus imposed onto peripheral countries, and in particular onto wage labourers, the self-employed, and small and medium businesses. The inequitable and strongly class-based nature of policies to confront the crisis was never in doubt.

Once the first shock was over, Germany fully exploited the opportunity presented by the crisis to determine the actions of the Troika. It took full advantage of its competitive superiority, its current account surpluses, and its creditor position to impose its will over the Eurozone, thus confirming its hegemony. It dictated the immediate steps to confront the crisis in the Southern periphery, imposed institutional policies presumably to restore competitiveness, altered the institutional structures of the EMU and the EU to suit its purposes, and systematically blocked all other proposals and suggestions. At the same time it continued to integrate the Central European periphery into its industrial exporting complex. By the end of the Eurozone crisis Germany had emerged as the dominant economic and political force of the EU.

In more detail the following four steps characterized the response of the Troika to the Eurozone.[7]

First, and decisively, the ECB began to provide liquidity to private and public banks in difficulties, driving interest rates close to zero. The process had already started in 2007–9 with the outbreak of the global crisis but assumed far greater dimensions after 2010. Command over the final means of payment by the

ECB was the most important lever in dealing with the Eurozone crisis, even though there is no single sovereign state behind the euro. This peculiarity of the common currency stamped the compromises through which the crisis was eventually pacified.

The overriding aim of ECB intervention in 2010–11 was to rescue the banks of the core – mainly German and French – that were exposed to the periphery of the EMU. Provision of liquidity took the form of the Securities Market Programme and included long-term refinancing operations in 2011, with the total sums being in the vicinity of 1 trillion euros. The policy was extended to Outright Monetary Transactions in 2012, allowing the ECB to purchase the public bonds of states in difficulties, but only in the secondary markets. That step signalled a significant relaxation of the rule that the central bank would not purchase the public debt of its member states.[8] However, the policy was never tested in practice as the pressure on the Eurozone abated soon after the announcement of the policy of Outright Monetary Transactions was made by the ECB.

The greatest increase in liquidity provision actually took place after 2015 in the form of quantitative easing that witnessed the ECB buying public bonds of all member states, though still in secondary markets. The balance sheet of the central bank expanded greatly and its liabilities rose to more than 3 trillion euros by 2016. Quantitative easing, quite apart from the vital support it gave to banks, also supported a gradual economic recovery across the EU, eventually allowing a return to mild growth by 2017. But the policies of the ECB created tensions with the Bundesbank since they have involved by-passing the rule that the central bank of the EMU would not purchase public debt, even if the purchases of the ECB were still not made in the primary markets. By 2017 the ECB (or, more accurately, the Eurosystem) had come to hold a tremendous stock of public debt securities from across the Eurozone in excess of 2 trillion euros. Its actions and the tensions that have arisen with the Bundesbank are evidence that Germany, although it has imposed its will on the EMU, still has to make compromises.

The second characteristic of the Troika's response to the crisis was the EU's consistent rejection of any prospect of debt forgiveness, or even substantial debt relief given to heavily indebted countries. This was despite the IMF clearly advocating debt relief to ease the pressure on stricken countries, especially Greece.[9] It has remained a principle of the EMU that no member state, and certainly not Germany, would accept direct responsibility for the debt of another. On the same grounds, Germany has systematically opposed all proposals to 'mutualize' debt, that is, jointly to share the risk of non-payment by a single state, through the issuing of Eurobonds, or similar instruments. However, the great stock of public bonds that the ECB has acquired represents a compromise in this respect too. For the risk attached to each individual bond reflects the creditworthiness of the state issuing it, and these risks have become partially submerged under the credit provided by the ECB, even if the bulk of these bonds are still held in practice by the Eurosystem, that is, by National Central Banks. The policy has driven interest rates down for member states of the EMU, and in practice the ECB carries some of the risk of state default.[10] Public debt might not have been 'mutualized' in the EMU, but it has to an extent become 'homogenized'. Germany hegemony has, once again, proven conditional.

Third, assistance was provided to states that could no longer access loanable funds in the international financial markets by creating ad hoc mechanisms of interstate lending. The critical steps in this respect were taken in 2010–11 as Greece, Portugal, and Ireland were shut out of the international financial markets. The EU was forced to create temporary mechanisms to provide funds since it possessed no permanent mechanisms for the purpose. Thus, the European Financial Stability Facility (EFSF) was created in 2010 which gradually led to the emergence of a permanent institutional framework to deal with this task, the European Stability Mechanism (ESM).

Creating the ESM was one of the most important institutional developments in the EU as a result of the crisis. The ESM is an unaccountable body, lacking entirely in democratic credentials, which commands substantial money funds, in the region of 500 billion euros, that are available for lending to countries in crisis. It has the power to impose severe 'conditionality' for the loans it makes, thus being able to impose a neoliberal agenda. By creating the ESM the EU could potentially develop its own IMF to act as the policing agent of neoliberal reform.[11]

Fourth, and crucially for growth and employment, debtor countries were obliged to achieve fiscal stability through the imposition of austerity, that is, by reducing public expenditure and raising taxes. There would be no backing down from this rule irrespective of the damage caused to employment, incomes, and production. At the same time, competitiveness would presumably be raised primarily through wage compression, privatization of public assets, and deregulation of markets. A neoliberal growth agenda, summed up in the official policy of 'Europe 2020', came to hold sway in the EU, complementing the dominance of austerity in public policy. The crisis was to be an opportunity to shift the class balance in favour of capital and against labour across the EU.

Beyond these measures taken to confront the immediate pressures of the crisis, the EU took a series of institutional steps to embed the principle of fiscal austerity in the EMU. The Stability and Growth Pact had manifestly failed to prevent the emergence of substantial deficits among peripheral and other countries by 2010. The Pact was supposed to impose sanctions on 'delinquent' countries but only after the emergence of 'excessive' deficits. In practice it had stopped acting as an effective disciplining mechanism already since 2005, when even France and Germany by-passed it. As the Eurozone crisis unfolded, the Pact was substantially hardened through a battery of legislative changes, including the Six Pack, the Two Pack, and the Fiscal Compact, the provisions of which include a restructured Excessive Deficit Procedure, the Macroeconomic Imbalances Procedure, and the European Semester.[12]

In typical bureaucratic fashion these reforms have created a wall of new institutions all with the plain aim of imposing fiscal austerity more effectively. The fundamental notion is that member states are to be administratively prevented from exceeding the targets for deficits, rather than having sanctions imposed on them after registering deficits. An environment of institutionalized austerity was created which accords the EU the right to impose penalties but also to police nation states if they fail to keep within the fiscal limits determined by the austerity principle. To this purpose the EU institutions, especially the Commission, have acquired fresh powers. Nevertheless, the byzantine complexity of these regulations raises serious doubts as to whether the rules would be adhered to in the short to medium term.

Broader neoliberal institutional reforms were also brought to bear with respect to banks. The ECB had already supported banks by providing liquidity, which in the periphery took the form of Emergency Liquidity Assistance, that is, a mechanism that allowed banks to borrow liquidity from their own National Central Banks at low rates of interest and with very weak collateral. However, there were also major problems of bank solvency owing to bad debts accumulated in the course of the crisis which threatened the existence of several banks. Historically, banks have required intervention by their nation states to deal with solvency problems and to forestall general bank failure.

To confront the problem of solvency the EU formed a Banking Union that includes the Single Supervisory Mechanism (SSM) and the Single Resolution Mechanism (SRM). The aim of the Banking Union is, presumably, to supersede the historical links between private banks and their respective nation states in dealing with the threat of bank failure. The SSM operates under the guidance of the ECB, and membership is compulsory for all EMU member-state banks but optional for EU member-state banks. The SSM has the power to perform stress tests on the balance sheet of banks, giving it the power to impose requirements of capital adequacy as well as to change the management of banks. The SRM, on the other hand, has jurisdiction over all banks under the SSM and is supposed to deal with failing banks. The plan is, presumably, for the EU to create some 'bailout' funds that would gradually be gathered through bank contributions. More important in the short term is the provision made to impose 'bailing-in', that is, to charge losses from bank failures to the owners of bank shares and bank bonds, and even to the holders of bank deposits. There is no realistic plan to create deposit insurance guarantees applying uniformly across the EMU and the EU, since that would impose substantial risks on the banks of one country for lending undertaken by the banks of another.

The banking reforms point to the class and national interests that have shaped EU policy in the crisis. Supervision of banks has been homogenized and now lies in the hands of the ECB, but the real test for banks always comes at the point of failure, that is, when fresh funds are required to keep them going, or the losses from failure have to be apportioned. The SRM represents a weak compromise in this regard, since it has not replaced the nation state with a transnational body that would have equivalent powers across the EU. Basically it proposes to shift the burden of insolvency onto the owners and the creditors of banks by making provision for 'bailing-in'. There is strong reason to believe that the provision would fail in the event of a crisis, especially if the threat of a general banking failure were to materialize. Once again, the reason for the compromise is that the EMU remains a treaty-based alliance in which no nation state, and certainly not Germany, would typically assume responsibility for the banks of another.

The Eurozone Crisis

An unstable and fraught equilibrium

The outcomes of EU policies were not difficult to foresee, and were indeed to a large extent foreseen.[13] The suppression of wages in the periphery and the severe fiscal austerity, especially in Greece and Spain, combined to cause a collapse of aggregate demand. Bank credit, meanwhile, suffered a sustained contraction as peripheral and core banks faced turmoil caused by accumulating bad debt. The result was a deep recession across the periphery that also affected the entire economy of the Eurozone. The impact on labour was catastrophic, with unemployment reaching unprecedented levels in Greece and Spain in 2012–13, especially among the young, before starting to decline around the middle of the decade. Huge unemployment exacerbated poverty, especially in view of the decline in public welfare provision as austerity spread. There is no doubt at all that the social costs of EU policies were borne primarily by wage labour and the young, especially in peripheral countries.

The main factor leading to recession was the decline in investment, which collapsed completely in the periphery. For Greece in particular the collapse of investment led to a historic retrogression of the economy. Given the austerity measures and the downward pressure on wages and pensions, consumption also came under acute pressure. The only boost to aggregate demand in the Eurozone during this period was provided by the ECB, particularly after quantitative easing began in 2015.[14]

Even so, it took years before the effect of quantitative easing was actually observed in growth rates. Only in 2017 did the economy of the Eurozone as a whole begin to register significantly positive growth. Moreover, the fundamental imbalances of the Eurozone have not been addressed. Figure 1 shows that wage repression in Germany has not been substantially lifted, even though nominal wage growth has accelerated compared to the 2000s. The gap in competitiveness between Germany and the Southern periphery has narrowed significantly as Greece and Spain have reduced wages, but it has not vanished. The core of the EMU is also riven with profound instability owing to the persistent gap in competitiveness between Germany, on the one hand, and France and Italy, on the other.

Some stability was nonetheless brought to the external transactions of the periphery. The elimination of current account deficits was due primarily to the collapse of imports as economies went into recession, while exports increased less. However, current account pressures on France have continued to accumulate as its competitiveness has suffered. Moreover, Italy is caught in a veritable trap since it has had weak productivity growth for a long time and the rise in exports is not sufficient to propel aggregate growth. Finally, austerity failed to deal with public debt, which was presumably one of the main concerns of EU policies. The ratio of public debt to GDP in both Spain and Greece increased substantially, and rapidly rising levels of public debt were registered in Italy and to a lesser extent in France.

By 2017 Germany had imposed its will on the EMU and the EU, pacifying the crisis within the confines of the EU. The dysfunctional regime of the euro was actually hardened, thus solidifying the advantages of German industrial exporting capital, particularly as Germany has refused even to consider changing its domestic policies. German exporting capital continued to earn enormous trading surpluses within the EU and across the world. Austerity and neoliberalism became the credo of the EU, while democratic rights suffered. Capital won at every major turn, while labour paid the price.

Neoliberal policies have wrought an economically unstable and politically fraught equilibrium in Europe. The notion of a common project of solidarity and unity among European people has been thoroughly discredited. A right-wing authoritarian wave has emerged, posing a major threat to the EU but also to social and political life in Europe. To determine its response the European Left ought to consider Greece, the country that has been the laboratory for EU economic, political, and social developments in the 2010s.

5

Greece in the Iron Trap
of the Euro

Greece found itself at the centre of the storm for most of the 2010s and the reason is not hard to find. The country displays in condensed form the main economic forces that led to the Eurozone crisis, the disastrous effects of the bail-outs, the class conflict at the roots of the turmoil, the international power-play that led to the institutional restructuring of the EMU and the EU, and the naked fact of German hegemony. It has been a veritable testing ground for theories and ideologies about Europe as well as a laboratory for European neoliberalism. If nothing else it shows what the European Left must avoid doing at all costs.

The proximate causes of the Greek crisis

The economic crisis that broke out in Greece in early 2010 was of a piece with the broader Eurozone turmoil, namely a 'sudden stop' crisis due to a balance of payments deficit combined with a large public debt owed mostly abroad.[1] Unfortunately, this realization came neither easily, nor naturally, to the EU. The policy-making apparatus of the union was initially convinced that there was nothing fundamentally wrong with the Eurozone, and Greece had caused its own problems by keeping 'dishonest' national statistics.

The initial response of the EU was thus vindictive, not least by imposing absurdly punitive interest rates on the loans that were urgently needed by the country in the spring of 2010. The aim was, presumably, to teach Greece – and other 'delinquent' countries – a moral lesson.[2] Gradually EU bureaucrats and politicians began to realize that things were rather more complicated, and that the crisis was systemic to the Eurozone. But a disparaging and haughty attitude never left the personnel of the Troika dealing with Greece in subsequent years. Arrogance comes easily to functionaries engaged in 'rescuing' crisis-stricken countries, and even more to politicians of core countries who ultimately make the policy decisions. The meekness, confusion, and subservience of the Greek side, meanwhile, confirmed the prejudices of the lenders.

The basic ingredients of the Greek crisis are by now clear. In the late 2000s the country registered an enormous current account deficit, a huge government deficit, and a very high ratio of public debt to GDP.[3] These elements came to a head in 2010, and international private lenders – mostly banks – became unwilling to advance fresh loans to the Greek state, seeking instead to recoup old loans. A 'sudden stop' materialized.

The crisis undoubtedly had domestic causes rooted in the unbalanced economy, the rapacious and inefficient state machine, and the exploitative and corrupt class structures that have marked Greece as a country since its inception. But these were long-standing historical causes and could never by themselves explain the sharpness and immensity of the crisis. For that it is necessary to turn to the country's membership of the EMU since 2001. The proximate cause of the Greek disaster was the euro.

Greece suffered a profound loss of national competitiveness during the 2000s, which accounted for the vast current account deficit as imports surged into the country, while public and private debt escalated. Why did Greek competitiveness decline so precipitously? The European Commission and many mainstream economists have no doubts on this score: the competitiveness of Greece declined because of its institutional weaknesses and the inefficiency of its economy and society.[4] The EU apparatus moved almost seamlessly from blaming Greek 'dishonesty' to blaming Greek 'inefficiency' and 'incompetence'. Inevitably the cure that it proposed involved a battery of neoliberal reforms of economy and society, presumably to restore competitiveness.

It is remarkable – and quite revealing of the nature of EU mechanisms – that in all the years that followed, even when it was apparent that the Greek 'rescue' was actually ravaging the country, the focus of the EU did not turn to the weighty factor of German wage and price policies. Greek nominal wages and the corresponding unit labour costs appeared to escalate in the 2000s, but mostly because German wages were effectively frozen, as was shown in Chapter 3. The deeper source of the problem for the Eurozone as a whole was German domestic policies, and Greek competitiveness collapsed with regard to the Eurozone as a whole. Furthermore, if Greece still had monetary sovereignty, the loss of competitiveness would have been confronted in the usual way, that is, by allowing the national currency, the drachma, to slide. But with the euro as its currency, Greece did not have that option. The country was trapped.

Essentially the same point could also be made in terms of the 'real exchange rate' of Greece, which recorded a substantial appreciation from the late 1990s to the late 2000s.[5] The main factors that explain the appreciation of the real exchange rate were, first, the higher rate of inflation of Greece compared to Germany and, second, the nominal appreciation of the euro compared to the dollar. The Greek current account deficit in the 2000s was mostly with its trade partners within the EMU, and was little affected by the rise of the euro relative to the dollar. The main factor behind the appreciation of the Greek 'real exchange rate' was higher inflation compared to Germany, which was closely correlated to unit labour costs that rose faster in Greece than in Germany. The Greek crisis might have had its roots at home, but its proximate causes were in the EMU.

Long-term weaknesses of the Greek economy

This is not in the slightest to deny the long-standing structural weaknesses of Greek capitalism.[6] There is no doubt that Greece has failed to compete successfully with its European 'partners' since joining the EEC in 1981, and nor is it in dispute that the structure of its economy has shifted disproportionately in favour of services at the expense of industry and agriculture. That was the background against which the loss of competitiveness in the 2000s led to the huge deficit in Greece's current account.[7]

Since the 1980s Greece has come to rely heavily on 'non-tradable' goods and services, that is, goods traded domestically rather than internationally.[8] Productivity has generally been low and consequently the country has imported ever larger proportions of high-technology products. The gravest weakness of the economy is in relation to the industrial sector, which depends heavily on imports. Whenever the rate of growth of the economy rises significantly, Greece faces strong 'leakages' abroad as imports grow faster than exports. The industrial sector, in particular, proved to be a black hole for external trade.

Greece has been in a developmental dead-end since joining the EEC. It has tended to specialize in low- and middle-technology commodities and has relied heavily on unskilled labour. Inevitably its productivity gains have been weak, which has made for limited growth potential of the economy as a whole. The low growth potential has been exacerbated by negative aggregate net saving ever since the country joined the EMU in 2001. Indeed, aggregate saving practically disappeared: net national saving in Greece has been systematically negative since the country's entry into the Eurozone.[9] The first decade of the country's membership of the Eurozone was marked by high consumption, relatively weak investment, and sustained trade deficits. For several years in the 2000s Greece actually registered fairly strong growth rates, for which it relied on being able to borrow from abroad. When foreign borrowing became impossible after the outbreak of the crisis in 2010, both growth and investment collapsed.

Joining the Eurozone in 2001 eventually brought the underlying tensions to a head. But the first few years of membership were marked by a false sense of prosperity that kept the country's social and political leadership unaware of the trap that had already shut. While competitiveness evaporated, private debt expanded greatly as Greek banks took advantage of cheap liquidity in the financial markets to expand loans. Strong growth in domestic demand and credit masked the underlying economic weakness. The Greek economy grew faster than Spain and Portugal, at rates often exceeding 4%.[10] There was even growth in investment in the late 1990s and 2000s, though it never reached the levels of Spain and Ireland.[11] Greek corporate investment as a proportion of GDP remained systematically lower than in other peripheral countries throughout the period.[12] The counterpart was a very high proportion of consumption relative to GDP, standing at above 70%, almost 10% higher than Portugal and even more compared to Spain, Italy, and Germany.[13]

There is no mystery regarding the dramatic increase in aggregate Greek debt – private and public, internal and external – in the 2000s. The more the country failed to compete within the Eurozone, the more its debt increased, both domestically and abroad. The escalation of indebtedness was a sign of fundamental economic weakness and loss of competitiveness.

Specifically, aggregate debt increased from roughly 150% in 1997 to a little less than 300% of GDP in 2009. More than 40% of aggregate debt was public, the highest proportion among peripheral countries, and two-thirds of the state's debt was owed abroad.[14] However, the fastest growing component of aggregate debt in the 2000s was private debt, especially by financial corporations and households. The growth of debt occurred as nominal and real interest rates declined rapidly in the periphery of the EMU after the adoption of the euro. Greek banks expanded their lending activities, but also relied heavily on domestic deposits and kept well away from derivatives and other forms of financial engineering. There was no credit bubble in Greece in the 2000s comparable to Spain or Ireland.[15]

Greece, similarly to other peripheral countries, borrowed heavily from abroad during the 2000s, and that has proved its downfall in the 2010s. The flows were spurred by Greek borrowers, primarily the state and the banks, and effectively financed the huge deficit in Greece's current account, also reflecting the country's negative saving. Foreign banks did not lead the rapid growth of credit in Greece. The culprit was burgeoning domestic credit expansion by Greek banks, which took advantage of the Eurozone to obtain liquidity cheaply. In a country that had lived with high nominal and real interest rates for decades, the low interest rate environment of the Eurozone offered unprecedented scope for credit expansion, much of it directed toward households. Historically and culturally, household debt has been frowned upon in Greece, but in the late 1990s and the 2000s households borrowed heavily to finance house purchases and consumption. The accumulation of household debt proved a major problem once the economy had been subjected to bail-out policies.

Public debt rose proportionately less than other parts of aggregate debt in the 2000s, but did so from an already high base compared to other peripheral countries. Relatively high public debt in Greece has its roots in the 1980s, reflecting in part the expansion of welfare provision at the time, and in part the sustained weaknesses of the tax system. Welfare provision in Greece has always been modest by Western European standards and there has long been systematic tax evasion. The economic and political power of large non-financial corporations and banks ensured relative tax immunity for the upper echelons of society. Significant tax evasion by the higher layers of self-employed professionals and small and medium enterprises was also widely tolerated.[16] Farmers, meanwhile, were historically given strong tax exemptions ostensibly for reasons of social policy.

Finally, Greek public debt in 2009 was overwhelmingly bond-based, denominated in euros, and governed by Greek law.[17] The international lenders had not done their work properly when it came to screening and monitoring their borrowers. As the spectre of default rose in 2010, the Greek state held a strong bargaining chip in its hands since it could unilaterally change the terms of debt repayment through an Act of Parliament. Unfortunately, it never used it.

When the global crisis of 2007–9 broke out, Greece sailed headlong into disaster. An unbalanced and uncompetitive economy laden with debt confronted a dysfunctional monetary union and a group of unyielding lenders, mostly German and French. The result was economic and social catastrophe.

The lenders impose bail-outs and bring disaster

The EU response to the Greek crisis was based on the accumulated experience of the IMF with 'sudden stop' crises in developing countries. But its application to Greece by the Troika offers fresh insights into how the approach works within a powerful monetary union.[18] Greece was provided with funding in the form of loans that it urgently needed, which came with 'conditionality' attached: that is, austerity policies to stabilize the external and the fiscal deficits as well as economic 'reforms', including deregulation of markets and privatization of public assets. 'Reforms' were particularly severe in the labour market, for instance, limiting trade union rights, abolishing collective bargaining, easing dismissals, intensifying the precariousness of employment, and so on. The lever for applying 'conditionality' was the gradual release of loan funds. If Greece complied, funds would be released; if it did not, funds would be withheld. Blackmail has rarely been more brazen.

IMF policies typically have enormous social costs, especially for the poorest, and they are also deeply problematic in terms of terms of growth, employment, income, and the productive structure of the economy. In Greece they proved entirely lethal. The reason was membership of the Eurozone, which created three crucial points of difference for the Greek economy.

The first, and less conspicuous, has to do with Greek banks, which lost enormous volumes of liquidity as the Greek public frantically withdrew its deposits. Nevertheless, the banks avoided the worst because they retained access to ECB liquidity. The ECB and the Eurosystem provided abundant liquidity to Greek banks through long-term refinancing operations, emergency liquidity assistance, and the TARGET2 settlement system.[19] The link between a balance of payments crisis and the emergence of a shortage of domestic liquidity was broken in the Greek case.[20]

Provision of ECB liquidity ensured that the Greek turmoil never became an acute banking crisis. At the same time, provision of liquidity gave the ECB a decisive lever of power over successive Greek governments. Greece avoided a banking collapse, thus remaining in the Eurozone, but on condition of submitting fully to the terms of 'conditionality'. The blackmail worked with the full connivance of Greek banks, which were desperate to continue receiving ECB liquidity. Banks have been the most powerful sectional interest within the country that has consistently pushed for full acceptance of the bail-out terms.

The second, and very visible, point was the absence of an exchange rate for Greece to devalue, thus helping the economy absorb the shock of the 'sudden stop'. Devaluation is not a long-term solution to the problem of low competitiveness as its impact would gradually and eventually pass onto domestic prices. But in the short term it could substantially lessen the pressures on the domestic economy, especially if the government also took tax and credit measures to support workers and enterprises.[21] Moreover, even in the long run, devaluation could create fresh fields for investment and production by sharply changing relative prices and improving the returns on domestic production. Greece had none of these benefits available to it since it clung to the euro.

The third, and equally visible, point was that Greece was availed of few options to restructure its public debt. Typical methods of debt relief would be to lower interest rates and extend the maturity of debt. A more decisive method would be to write off some of the principal of the loans, thus also reducing the pressure of refinancing the debt.[22] There is undeniable evidence that the IMF was fully aware of the importance of Greek debt restructuring in 2010, but debt relief, and especially writing off debt, was rejected out of hand by Eurozone lenders.[23] The reason was that a major Greek debt restructuring in 2010 would have entailed substantial losses for the lenders, posing grave risks for Eurozone banks but also for the very survival of the monetary union. From the perspective of the lenders, if Greece wished to remain in the Eurozone, it had to bear the brunt of the adjustment without debt restructuring.

Eurozone membership has devastated Greece in the 2010s. The self-interest and arrogance of its 'partners' has been more than matched by the venality and cowardice of its own ruling elite. The country received its first bail-out in May 2010, with the Greek state explicitly committing itself to servicing its existing debt, thus avoiding default.[24] The programme was 'front-loaded', meaning that there would be great cuts in public expenditure for the initial period, followed by substantial increases in taxes at a later time. A full set of 'conditionality' conditions were also specified.

The Greek bail-out agreement of 2010 is one of the worst documents on economic policy ever drafted. It bore no relation either to the realities of the Greek economy, or to the likely impact of the proposed policies. The magnitude of the fiscal adjustment imposed on the country was enormous, as were the external deficit and the competitiveness gap that had to be closed. The adjustment had to occur within the iron trap of the EMU, without depreciation or debt relief. IMF economists have officially admitted that their estimates of the likely effects of their programme on the Greek economy were entirely baseless.[25] When their 'cure' was applied, disaster followed.

Aggregate demand contracted violently, and output fell by nearly 7% in both 2011 and 2012, the total contraction exceeding 25% in 2008–16. The deepest fall was in investment as enterprises reacted to the decline in demand, but also to the tighter credit conditions given that banks had growing volumes of problematic public debt on their balance sheets. Equally bad for enterprises, but much less noticed, was the effective disappearance of commercial credit. The collapse in output dramatically increased adult unemployment, which exceeded 27% in 2013.

It was apparent already by the middle of 2011 that the first bail-out programme had backfired badly. Above all, the recession had worsened the ratio of public debt to GDP, and Greece continued to face severe difficulties in servicing its debt. The country needed a new bail-out and urgent debt restructuring. By that time, however, the balance of political forces in Europe had significantly changed compared to early 2010. For one thing, European banks had begun substantially to disengage themselves from Greece already in 2010. For another, as noted in the previous chapter, the EU had taken steps to establish a panoply of institutions to confront sovereign debt problems, including the European Financial Stability Facility, which eventually became the European Stability Mechanism. The risks arising from a Greek default and exit from the EMU had been attenuated.

In 2012 Greece received a second bail-out with attached 'conditionality'. Furthermore, during 2011–12 the country was afforded some debt restructuring which was remarkable for its one-sided and limited nature. Greece was offered extended periods of grace for the bail-out loans, a reduction in average interest rates by granting the fresh funds at concessional rates, and a lengthening of the average maturity of debt.[26] Some of the principal of the Greek debt was also written off, the so-called 'private sector involvement' (PSI). Thus, in 2012 Greece implemented a bond swap and subsequently a debt buy-back that resulted in nominal debt relief of more than 100 billion euros.[27]

Unfortunately for Greece, the losses from PSI fell heavily on domestic rather than foreign lenders, the latter escaping with relatively limited damage. Greek banks in particular were badly affected since they held substantial volumes of government debt, and the country was forced to use a large part of the bail-out funds for bank recapitalization. The Greek PSI was a monument to callousness and self-interest on the part of the lenders, as well as to subservience and shortsightedness on the part of the borrower. There cannot have been many other historical instances of sovereign default which have hurt domestic more than foreign lenders. Moreover, the bail-out funds eventually changed the composition of Greek public debt away from bonds governed by Greek law and toward bilateral or multilateral state debt, governed by international law.[28] The country had lost its main bargaining chip without ever using it.

Finally, in 2015 Greece required a third bail-out, following a significant political upheaval that is discussed in the rest of this chapter. The underlying cause was much the same: the economy had contracted and public debt was impossible to service. The 'conditionality' attached to the third bail-out was of a similar nature, but by 2015 much of the fiscal and the external adjustment of the country had already been accomplished by impoverishing both economy and society. The pressing problem for Greece in the mid-2010s had become the achievement of sustainable growth and development rather than stabilization.

The bail-outs failed decisively to improve the country's competitiveness, and did not create prospects of sustained growth and rising employment. Greece has remained firmly lodged in the Southern periphery and faces long-term weakness. In one of those bitter paradoxes of history, the determination of its rulers to keep it in the EMU, and thus at the putative heart of European integration, meant that the country, after years of shrinkage and decline, has returned to the Balkans in terms of economic size and influence.

To be more specific, Greek exports have shown little dynamism over time, and as soon as the economy registers a positive rate of growth, the tendency toward a widening external deficit tends to reappear as imports increase. Investment has completely collapsed, standing at barely above 10% of GDP in 2017, and matching the negative net saving of the country. Unemployment, meanwhile, remained in the vicinity of 21% in 2017, despite the rapid growth of part-time and precarious employment in the service sector, and the large-scale emigration of trained youth. Greece, which has a very weak population growth, has squandered its labour resources on a grand scale in the 2010s.

At the same time, public debt stood in the vicinity of 180% of GDP in 2017, and was manifestly unsustainable. A country that was thrown into a crisis because of its inability to service its public debt came out of it with a dramatically worsened ratio of debt to GDP. Furthermore, the Greek banking system, which became heavily concentrated in the course of the bail-outs, faced a tremendous accumulation of non-performing loans and other exposure, reaching 45% of total assets in 2017. In effect Greece no longer possessed a functioning banking system that could support capitalist accumulation and growth.

The long-term prospects of the Greek economy were thus poor. The competitiveness gap was partially closed owing to the collapse of nominal (and real) wages in 2010–13, but stopped narrowing already in 2013–14. Moreover, the structure of the economy remained fundamentally unchanged with heavy predominance of services, a small and weak industrial sector with a pronounced propensity to import, and an agricultural sector with low productivity and low competitiveness. The long-term weaknesses of the economy were not tackled at all, and growth prospects looked dim, especially in view of the loss of hundreds of thousands of skilled young workers to emigration.

Finally, the administrative capabilities of the Greek state were not materially improved by the bail-out policies; indeed they might have even declined in some areas as there was loss of employment in the civil service, real wages declined, and morale collapsed. To make matters worse, the power of the lenders was continually manifested through the presence of the Troika in several key locations within the state. Not a single economic or social decision could be made by the Greek state without the agreement of the Troika. Greek sovereignty drained away dramatically.

In the late 2010s the future of Greece in the Eurozone looks bleak. The country has gone through a period of tremendous economic contraction with acute social implications, including a rapid increase in poverty, a decline in primary health care, deep cuts in resources for educational institutions, and escalating homelessness and shared housing. It faces years of low and unstable growth, with large unemployment, persistent poverty, and continuing social dislocation. The political counterpart to economic weakness is the emergence of a state machine that is incapable of exercising sovereignty over key areas of policy, and is subservient to the demands of the lenders. Such has been the price of Greece remaining in the iron trap of the euro.

Class and national interests in the Greek disaster

The stance of the Troika and the lenders toward Greece is not hard to explain. Neoliberal ideology holds powerful ideological sway among EU governments, institutions, and bureaucrats, and of course in the IMF. The dominant political role in shaping the lenders' approach to Greece was played by Germany, a country with an entrenched ideological belief that its 'success' in the 2000s was due to the painful reforms of the 1990s and 2000s. The political message emanating from Berlin was that Germany was the model for the EMU, and therefore austerity and 'reforms' were the appropriate policy for Greece, the Southern periphery, and the EU more generally.[29]

In the realm of material class interests the priority of the Troika was to protect the lenders from losses and the Eurozone from the threat of a major rupture, as the IMF has openly admitted.[30] Any other course of action in Greece in 2010–11, especially if it had included default and exit from the EMU, would have caused major material damage to the banks of the core, but also to the Eurozone. Germany was not prepared to countenance the risk to its conditional hegemony that this action would have posed at the time. Greece had to be prevented from defaulting and exiting, while submitting to the bail-out programmes.

As the crisis unfolded in the early 2010s the attitude of the EU toward Greece changed considerably, not least because of the institutions created – above all the ESM – which appeared capable of dealing with crises. At the same time the EU hardened the institutional regime of the Eurozone through fiscal discipline and neoliberal reform. Already in 2012 the lenders could contemplate with relative equanimity the prospect of a Greek default and exit from the EMU.

Equally significant was the change in the position of the IMF in the course of the crisis. The Greek programme was rightly perceived as a failure, which, moreover, led to substantial financial exposure of the Fund to Greece. The IMF clashed with the EU on the question of 'conditionality', which the EU bureaucrats intended to make highly intrusive, attempting to reshape Greek society and the Greek state. The aim of the IMF, in contrast, was primarily to achieve macroeconomic stabilization. The difference is important and telling. The IMF is a multilateral organization that speaks for global capitalist interests, and is not in the business of reshaping EU member states. The main force for the neoliberal hardening of the EU in the course of the crisis was the EU itself, led by Germany. Its mechanisms prevailed over the IMF and insisted that detailed 'reform' measures should be applied to Greece and the periphery, often in direct opposition to national authorities.[31]

The shifting attitude of the IMF became apparent in the third Greek bail-out in 2015, in which the Fund did not officially participate as a lender. The IMF argued strongly that Greek debt was not sustainable and the severe austerity imposed on Greece was incompatible with the debt. The Fund actually advocated deep restructuring of Greek debt, with a concomitant relaxation of fiscal austerity in the medium term. The EU would not concur since any losses on Greek debt would be borne directly by public institutions in Europe, thus creating political and electoral repercussions. Hegemonic interests prevailed, denying Greece deep debt relief for the foreseeable future.

If the attitude of the lenders presents few analytical problems, the attitude of the borrower is a real conundrum. Why did Greece in 2010 accept a programme that was manifestly defective, and why has it persevered with bail-outs for several years in spite of the damage wrought to its economy and society? What are the class interests that have dictated this course of action, and what are the implications for sovereignty and the national standing of the country? To find answers it is important to focus on the Greek 'historical bloc', to use Gramsci's well-known term: in other words the alliance of dominant sections of the capitalist class with lower classes that plays a hegemonic role in the economy, politics, and culture of a country.[32]

It is not necessary here to engage in a sociological description of the Greek historical bloc during the decades following the country's accession to the EEC in 1981. Suffice it to state that the dominant capitalist elements have included ship-owning, banking, construction, and manufacturing, which also have widespread ownership and control over the mass media. These class interests have had great influence over the state machine, translating into privileged access to public procurement and institutionalized tax avoidance.

The Greek state in the post-war decades followed its own long historical tradition of deploying the forms of a democratic polity, while in practice treating society as an occupied territory for the purposes of tax and welfare provision.[33] The resulting mechanisms of integration and social control revolved around party patronage, a characteristic feature of the Greek social formation since the middle of the nineteenth century. The historical bloc that emerged in the post-war years also included the upper layers of the professional self-employed, parts of the small and medium business stratum, and some of the larger agrarian landholders, all of whom secured variable tax and other privileges through a complex electoral machine connected to political parties and the state.

The vital point to grasp about the Greek historical bloc in the face of the crisis of 2010 is not what it decided *to do* but rather what it was absolutely determined *not to do*. And that was to exit the EMU. There can be no doubt on this score since the determination to remain in the EMU at all costs was restated countless times by government officials and others, not to mention being confirmed by the practice of several Greek governments. For the Greek historical bloc, staying in the EMU became an article of faith. Consequently, successive Greek governments accepted dealing with the crisis without having command over monetary and exchange rate policy. They also accepted that fiscal policy would be rigidly determined by the Troika, credit policy would be increasingly set by the Banking Union, and trade policy would be shaped by a series of EU directives.

The vicious nature of the Greek crisis resulted largely from this dramatic loss of sovereignty and the lack of command over economic policy instruments. The only option available to Greek governments after 2010 was to attempt to change particular details of the bail-out programmes while complaining about the attitude of the Troika. The exception was the first SYRIZA government, elected in January 2015 on a platform of radical policy change. When that government capitulated and signed the third bail-out in August the same year, Greece returned to its previous stance.

But why has the Greek historical bloc acceded to a programme that has profoundly damaged the country? What explains the extraordinary – and extraordinarily destructive – determination to remain in the iron trap of the euro almost regardless of economic and political cost?

Part of the explanation relates to sectional economic interests within the bloc, notably the Greek banks. Without sustained ECB liquidity provision and without access to bail-out funds for recapitalization, Greek banks would have been forced to suspend operations as well as facing possible nationalization. Quite naturally they were the strongest and most unwavering supporters of bail-out programmes in Greece. The ability of banks to impose their will was considerably increased by control over political parties and the mass media, both of which were heavily indebted to them. Much harder to explain is the acquiescence of Greek industrial and manufacturing capital, particularly the construction sector. As investment collapsed, the productive sector of Greece faced destruction of historic dimensions. To account for the acquiescence of productive capitalists to bail-out policies it is necessary to mobilize broader arguments about the power structures of Greek society and the political outlook and culture of the Greek people.

One important factor was plain fear. Default and exit would have led to economic and social turmoil in the short term that could have generated profound political unrest. In such circumstances it would have been impossible to predict which political forces would emerge to challenge for power. This was a risk that the Greek historical bloc was not prepared to take. From this perspective it was a rational decision to accept the path of the bail-outs and the attendant loss of sovereignty rather than risk a deep upheaval. Fear of default and exit has become an entrenched part of Greek public debate since the early 2010s, cultivated assiduously by mass media outlets typically owned by powerful business interests. Legions of outlandish claims were made of the destruction that was likely to follow, including food shortages, lack of medicines, and violent unrest in the streets with looting and arson. Fear assumed the dimensions of a political force.

Equally important, however, was the notion of identity attached to the euro. Money, after all, is an integral part of national and social identity.[34] The euro in Greece has come to symbolize a 'European' outlook that overcomes national divisions and is associated with modernity, progress, and the future. In a small peripheral country that has historically identified 'progress' with developments in Western Europe, these were very powerful ideological factors. Abandoning the euro and reintroducing a national currency would appear to be stepping backward and weakening the 'European' character of the Greek people.[35] These arguments, relentlessly cultivated by the intellectual elite of the country, much of it resident in its universities, acquired extraordinary purchase and led to an astonishing uniformity of thought in the public domain.[36]

These were the crucial issues on which class conflict crystallized in Greece as the bail-out policies wrought havoc to economy and society in the early 2010s. The Greek historical bloc, placing its own class interests ahead of those of society, preferred to accept a severe loss of sovereignty by submitting to the lenders, even if that meant accepting wholesale economic destruction for the nation. Under no circumstances would the bloc contemplate defaulting on the national debt and exiting the EMU. This momentous decision entailed enormous damage for the country and has placed it on a path of long-term economic and social decline.

The political débâcle of SYRIZA

The political fears of the Greek historical bloc were well justified. Mass reaction against the bail-out measures did occur in 2011–12, particularly with the movement to 'Occupy the Squares' of Greek towns and cities, especially Syntagma Square in Athens, the political heart of Greece. The mass reaction of the Greek people also turned against the corrupt and incompetent political system that had brought the country to its knees.

However, popular reaction failed to give birth to an independent movement separate from political parties. Instead it took electoral form and the main beneficiary was SYRIZA, until then a tiny and untried party of the Left.

SYRIZA had very limited connections to the established mechanisms of power in Greek politics and the state, and spoke the language of wholesale reform and even rebellion in Greece and Europe. It posed a real and present threat to the Greek mechanisms of power, and provided a vehicle for the anger of the Squares, particularly as its young leader, Alexis Tsipras, seemed fresh, radical, and daring. Unfortunately, reality would prove that youth is a guarantee of neither radicalism nor daring in politics.

SYRIZA enjoyed a tremendous groundswell of popular support after 2012 and won power in January 2015. It then engaged in protracted negotiations with the lenders. By August 2015 it was thoroughly defeated and had surrendered wholesale, signing up to Greece's third bail-out. It became yet another Greek party, applying the harsh terms of the new bail-out, while playing the traditional game of patronage and petty politicking characteristic of the country. 'Normal' politics returned in Greece, except that this time the government called itself of the Left.

The surrender and about-turn of SYRIZA is truly a dark chapter in the history of the European Left. The first step in accounting for it is to consider the outlook of the Greek working and lower middle classes. For, in contrast to the historical bloc of Greece, the attitude of the lower classes was far more fluid and ready to countenance even the option of default and exit. Despite the sustained campaign of fear, opinion polls have consistently shown that between a fifth and a third of the Greek population, mostly its poorest layers, support these options.

The class lines were sharply drawn in Greece as soon as the Greek historical bloc made clear its determination to comply with paying the debt and remaining in the EMU under any circumstances. For workers and the poor these two issues touched directly on popular and national sovereignty. The plebeian layers were prepared to contemplate radical steps. To find political leadership they instinctively and immediately looked to the Left, and that is where the problem lay.

The largest organization of the Greek Left has traditionally been the Communist Party, the KKE. It would be an understatement to say that the KKE proved irrelevant to the Greek turmoil. The party failed entirely to propose a political programme that would confront the key class questions of the crisis, that is, the debt and the euro. Instead, it sought refuge in ultra-leftism, largely implying that the Greek crisis could be dealt with only by overturning capitalism, a step that would naturally take the country out of the EU and the EMU. The party was always quick to add, however, that leaving the EMU, or even the EU, without 'popular power' would be disastrous for Greece. By taking this position the KKE effectively neutralized itself as a political force, and posed practically no danger to the Greek historical bloc throughout the crisis.

In the absence of the KKE, SYRIZA found propitious terrain. The roots of its eventual débâcle lay in a political division within the party which had a long pedigree and emerged with particular sharpness in the course of the crisis. On one side, the leadership of SYRIZA, coalescing around Alexis Tsipras and a narrow group of his own personal allies, adopted the strategy of reversing austerity, raising wages, and achieving substantial debt restructuring through 'tough negotiations' with the European lenders. It began to promise to the Greek people that it would 'tear up' the bail-out agreements, while also keeping the country in the EMU and avoiding a break with the EU. The lenders would presumably relent in the face of the democratic legitimacy of a new SYRIZA government, and thus SYRIZA would also help change the face of Europe. This strategy drew partly on the long-standing current of Europhilism within the Greek Left, and mostly on cold-headed electoral calculation.

Opposing Tsipras was a vocal and influential minority, coalescing around the so-called 'Left Platform', which actually was one of the founding constituents of SYRIZA. The minority was powerfully represented across the party, including in its upper echelons. It was essentially the left wing of SYRIZA, which advocated unilateral default and exit from the EMU by drawing on a long-standing ideological tradition of the Greek Left, close to the KKE. The minority clearly appreciated the dead-end which the strategy of the leadership actually represented, and argued for default and exit.[37]

Needless to say there were many more eddies and swirls of political opinion and organization within SYRIZA, some of which played an important role in the unfolding of events. But the path of the party and thus of the country itself was determined by the contest between these two main currents. Of crucial importance was that the struggle took place primarily within parliamentary and party mechanisms rather than in the streets, neighbourhoods, and workplaces of Greece. This simple fact, together with the organizational and political weaknesses of the Left Platform, proved pivotal to the eventual victory of the leadership. Finally, it should be mentioned that the Finance Minister of SYRIZA, Yanis Varoufakis, who did not belong to the party's left wing, indeed did not even hail from the Left altogether, contributed avidly to the analytical confusion that led to the débâcle.[38]

The leadership's strategy was tried immediately after SYRIZA's electoral victory on 25 January 2015, and its failure was total and irrevocable. Indeed, the strategy could not even survive the first contact with the Troika. The Greek team was led by Varoufakis, who had joined the leadership before the election, and became one of the architects of its strategy. Varoufakis's negotiating approach was that Greece should assume a hard stance by refusing to accept fresh loans while demanding substantial debt relief, a partial lifting of austerity, and a modification of Troika 'reforms'. Varoufakis was adamant that Greece should remain in the EMU, but also insisted that it should not budge from its demands on the lenders, even at the risk of being expelled.

How the Greek negotiating team could maintain these deeply contradictory positions simultaneously was entirely unclear. Perhaps Varoufakis hoped that the threat of potential disruption in the global markets would force the lenders into concessions. He also seemed to lay great store by a possible Greek threat unilaterally to write off some of the country's (proportionately negligible) debt to the ECB. Apparently that unilateral action would have created insuperable legal complications in Germany, potentially forcing the ECB to abandon quantitative easing.

There is no need to weigh these arguments any further, however, as events speak for themselves. At the first Eurogroup meeting attended by the new government, held on 11 February 2015, the lenders were implacable and demanded full compliance with the existing bail-out conditions. The SYRIZA side did not just lose the battle, it suffered a complete rout.[39] In an agreement signed on 20 February, Varoufakis agreed fully to honour the country's obligations with regard to debt and to desist from unilateral actions. When that first and crucial bout of negotiations was over, Tsipras's' government had effectively agreed to scrap the programme on which it had been elected, and the Finance Minister presided over a ruined negotiating strategy. The ground had been set for the final surrender in August.

The infamous deal of 20 February led to an internal revolt by the left wing of SYRIZA, which voted to reject it in a closed session of the party's parliamentary group. Tsipras found himself in a difficult position since he was in direct danger of losing his parliamentary majority. Able old-school politician that he is, however, he managed to manipulate the dissent within his party and never brought the agreement to be ratified in Parliament. Working in cahoots with his Finance Minister, he chose to remain on the path that the lenders had laid out for SYRIZA and the country, for to have taken another path would have required preparing for rupture with the lenders and exiting the EMU. It would also have required mass popular mobilization in Greece and a sharpening of domestic class opposition to the point of breaking the power of the Greek historical bloc. Alexis Tsipras is not made of such stuff.

After the agreement of 20 February there followed several months of hopeless further negotiations with the lenders, who had fully realized the weakness and incoherence of the SYRIZA side, and soon forced Tsipras to side-line Varoufakis, even if formally retaining him as Finance Minister. Much further posturing took place and even, apparently, some last-minute attempts by Varoufakis to devise a secret plan for a euro-denominated parallel currency issued by the Greek state, which could have potentially led to a Greek exit from the EMU. But the lenders won every single battle. There are two fundamental reasons for their triumph, both of which are of crucial importance for the European Left.

The first is the rigid institutional structure of the EMU, which became even more unyielding in the course of the crisis. The leading institutions of the EMU possess ample means to destroy opposition within the monetary union. Their ultimate weapon is the monopoly power of the ECB over the final means of payment and the provision of liquidity. As soon as SYRIZA was elected, the ECB began to restrict the supply of liquidity to the Greek economy and gradually brought the country to a state of asphyxiation. The SYRIZA government could find no effective answer to the ECB's policy because none was available within the confines of the EMU. The only possible answer would have been to create national liquidity, that is, to exit the EMU. But this would have involved adopting the rebellious domestic and international path advocated by the left-wing opposition within SYRIZA.

At bottom, membership of the EMU is an issue of class and national power that cannot be confronted by clever technical plans hatched by economists, much less by ill-thought-out schemes to issue a parallel euro-denominated currency. Tackling exit would have required actively building mass support and preparing to confront the violent reaction of domestic and foreign interests. The SYRIZA leadership would have none of that. It complained, dallied, retreated, attempted to buy time by soaking up all available domestic liquidity, and in the end surrendered.

The second reason is the absolute ideological hostility of the mechanisms of the EU and the EMU toward left-wing ideas and policies. It would have been unthinkable for the neoliberal machinery at the core of Europe to give any leeway to a government of radical upstarts who barely appreciated how the institutions of Europe actually worked. The hostility never abated until SYRIZA was finally defeated. The point is crucial for those on the Left who still harbour notions of radical change in the EU through mere electoral means. The core of the EU showed complete disregard for the wishes of the Greek people and paid no heed to democracy.

That disregard was graphically manifested in the Greek referendum of July 2015 held over the question of whether the country should accept the harsh terms of the Troika. The class lines were sharply drawn, with the Greek elite being four-square for Yes, and, with the full support of the lenders, engaging in a frantic campaign of misinformation and scare-mongering about being thrown out of the EMU. The plebeian layers of Greek society were adamantly in favour of No. In the event the great majority of the Greek people voted No, showing that, despite all, they were ready for a fight against the lenders to defend social integrity and reclaim sovereignty. But the SYRIZA leadership had neither the historical stature, nor the required strategy to carry the popular will. Tsipras cynically turned No into Yes, and became an obedient tool of the lenders by fully signing up to a new bail-out. Unfortunately the left wing of SYRIZA did not have the strength and the organization to win the internal fight.

The surrender of Alexis Tsipras and his party, apart from being a shameful historical event, shows precisely the strategy that the European Left *must not* adopt. The Left must not try to implement policies that are against austerity and in favour of working people while also attempting to stay in the EMU. There can be no disobedience from within, no 'creative ambiguity' in negotiations, no attempt to force the mechanisms of the EMU to relent by relying on democratic authority. This is a hopeless path that leads to certain defeat. A left government must instead prepare for rupture with the EMU, and for a direct challenge to and even rejection of the EU. That is the only positive lesson for the European Left from the débâcle of SYRIZA.

6

Seeking Democracy, Sovereignty, and Socialism

Democracy and sovereignty in the EU, once again

The Greek crisis provides clear evidence of the hollowing out of democracy in the EU as neoliberalism has marched on relentlessly. The democratic defects of the EU have been known for a long time, and reference was made earlier in this book to the academic debate on the 'crisis of representation'. There is a similarly broad academic debate on the 'democratic deficit' of the EU, which is best summed up in terms of 'input' and 'output' factors, that is, in terms of the weaknesses of the process of decision making in the EU and its outcomes.[1] The crisis of the Eurozone and the turmoil of the 2010s have severely aggravated the democratic deficit of the EU.

The structural problem is not hard to see. For one thing, the bodies of the EU's 'executive' – that is, the Commission, the Council, and a host of other committees – are neither properly elected nor fully accountable to an elected body. They are ultimately appointed by the heads of member states and their authority is delegated.

113

The decision taken in 2014 that the appointment of the President of the Commission must be approved by the European Parliament represents a largely cosmetic change in this regard because the real power to appoint still lies with member states.

For another thing, the 'legislature' of the EU – that is, the Council of Ministers and the Parliament – is either not elected at all (i.e. the Council) or elected through a political process that is not remotely comparable to domestic national politics (i.e. the Parliament). There are, of course, elections for the European Parliament, but these are not an arena for ideological political contestation reflecting social interests, as happens in national elections.

European Parliamentary elections are profoundly 'depoliticized', and the reasons are integral to the EU. National parliamentary elections are occasions for the *demos* to express its collective will, and in capitalist societies the *demos* is inseparable from its class and other divisions. National democratic politics is a contest among social interests vying for electoral supremacy, which may take a conscious class form and thereby acquire a characteristic sharpness, bitterness, and rivalry. There is, however, no European *demos*.[2] No class or other social divisions in Europe take a homogeneous 'European' form, for there are no occupational, organizational, habitual, cultural, and historical norms able to create such an overarching social integration. Actual class divisions in Europe always take a national form, as do the party politics that correspond to these divisions. In Marxist terms there is neither a European capitalist class nor a European working class. Both classes are irreducibly national, though the meaning of 'being national' differs profoundly between them, as is shown below.

This is in no way to deny the cultural affinities and the shared historical experiences of European people. Even less is it to negate the possibility of transnational solidarity and support among the working classes of Europe. The commonality of aspirations, hopes, and objectives among working people is not predicated upon ignoring their national differences. There is no need to proclaim a 'global' working class to ensure international solidarity among workers. Analogously, there is cooperation among capitalist classes across Europe, especially when it comes to sustaining the neoliberal project of the EU, but there are also insuperable national divisions, hierarchy and hegemony among them.

The absence of a European *demos* with its integral class divisions prevents the existence of 'normal' politics in the EU. There are no social cleavages applying uniformly across EU member states that could be organically reflected in political contestation within EU institutions. For essentially the same reason, there are no 'European' parties in the European Parliament, but rather heterogeneous coalitions with considerable programmatic overlaps among them. Conflict lines in the European Parliament are often between countries rather between social groups. In this respect there could be no analogy between EU and national politics. The EU certainly adopts several forms and practices of democracy, but these do not correspond to the aspirations and demands of overarching social forces with their inherent divisions. For this reason the European Parliament, in spite of the formal practices it adopts, is peculiarly devoid of politics, as is obvious in comparison with any national parliament. The absence of politics is part and parcel of the democratic deficit of the EU, since democracy in a capitalist society is about class-based political contestation.

The implications are crucial for the 'judiciary' of the EU, that is, for the bodies interpreting and applying the vast *acquis communautaire*. The *acquis* has not resulted from a democratic political process similar to that found in several European countries which involves contest and accountability in making laws. Rather, it represents a *de facto* accretion of laws that derive whatever legitimacy they have from the power of the bodies that have promulgated them. In a profound sense the *acquis* lacks democratic credentials and is suspended by its own bootstraps, and for this reason is extremely important to the single market. The *acquis* is an enormous body of legislation that is self-standing, remote from democratic processes, and able to act as a seemingly independent guarantor of the functioning of the single market.

Given the importance of the *acquis*, the European Court of Justice (ECJ) has gradually elevated itself into the enforcer of the neoliberal transformation of the EU. Particularly since the Maastricht Treaty, the rulings of the ECJ have crucially influenced the ability of member states to formulate national policies. In particular the freedom to adopt social policies has been heavily constrained by the requirement to comply with the concept of economic efficiency embedded in the *acquis* and interpreted through the prism of neoliberalism.[3] A veritable machine has been created for the relentless application of neoliberal ideology across Europe, which demands 'harmonization' of national legislation on the presumption of the superiority of EU law and at the cost of hefty

116

fines. In the words of a legal authority: 'According to this conception of rights of the European Courts, priority should be assigned to the rights of capital holders over the socio-economic rights affirmed in most of the fundamental laws of the Member States of the European Union (including, above all, collective fundamental rights and collective fundamental goods).'[4]

The ECJ is arguably the strangest institution in a veritable menagerie of strange institutions in the EU. It evidently lacks the democratic legitimacy afforded to national constitutional courts through the usual democratic political process, and nor is it subject to similar constraints of accountability. Its authority is delegated to it by member states that have willingly curtailed their judicial sovereignty in favour of the ECJ. And yet the ECJ is typically considered superior to national judiciaries, a profoundly paradoxical state of affairs since its authority derives ultimately from the actions of a collection of states.[5] The paradox allows the ECJ to enforce neoliberal policies across the EU by consistently deciding in favour of further European integration and interpreting the *acquis* accordingly, particularly in relation to the Four Freedoms of the EU and European competition law. Member states accept the supremacy of this guardian of the single market as long as it is politically expedient for all to support the neoliberal transformation of the EU.

In the course of the Eurozone crisis the democratic deficit of the EU became notably worse.[6] Supranational EU institutions, including the Commission, the European Parliament, and the ECB, acquired further powers to impose neoliberal reforms, while also supervising member states.[7] Democratic controls over economic

117

policy were attenuated to the extent that the expressly declared popular will was deliberately by-passed in several countries, and nowhere more than in Greece. At the same time, core states sitting in Council, or participating in the extraordinary bodies empowered by the EU to deal with the crisis, such as the Eurogroup and Eurogroup Working Group, also enhanced their power. None benefited more than Germany. Peripheral countries lost out and their loss of sovereignty translated directly into a decline of democracy. Labour also lost out as its conditions worsened relative to capital across the EU.

The damage wrought by the Eurozone crisis to the democratic credentials of the EU and the crucial role played by the absence of a European *demos* in the evolution of the EU became sharply visible during the refugee and migrant crisis that erupted in 2015. It is worth briefly digressing on this issue since it casts a sharp light on the moral outlook of the EU as well as on the hollowing out of democracy. Waves of desperate people, mostly from war-torn Syria, crossed the Aegean Sea from Turkey to Greece seeking passage primarily to Germany, Sweden, and Denmark. Their numbers were not dramatic but their plight certainly was. If any of the highfalutin notions about the EU were actually true, the refugees ought to have been treated in accordance with EU law, consensus, and institutional solidarity. Reality proved vastly different.

The legal framework for dealing with the issue was provided by the so-called 'Dublin regulations', which have been amended and changed several times. They basically state that, when an asylum seeker enters the EU, legal responsibility lies with the member state where the asylum seeker first entered.[8] If asylum seekers were found in other member states, they could be deported to where they first entered. As hundreds of thousands of refugees crossed to Greece in 2015, the country was overwhelmed, especially since it was already in the throes of a devastating economic crisis. It soon became clear that the true aim of the EU was to staunch the flows by preventing the refugees from reaching the core of Europe. They were to be kept trapped either outside the EU, as in Turkey, or within the EU, as in Greece.

Disgraceful events followed as Europe could not bring itself to admit a relatively small number of destitute people. There was no integrated policy, and indeed the EU response was soon fragmented along national lines aiming either to keep refugees out, or to admit as many as a willing national economy was expected to accommodate. Right-wing political opposition to refugee entry resonated with broad layers of the population of several countries, drawing on concerns about welfare provision and cultural fears. Member states acted on the basis of their own prerogatives, effectively signalling the supremacy of national legislation when states chose to apply it. The route to Central Europe from Greece was blocked as Hungary closed its borders to asylum seekers, and other countries took similar measures. Germany activated its own national legislation and unilaterally admitted one million refugees. Other large EU countries, including France and Britain, admitted only negligible numbers. The only factor that rescued the dignity of Europe was a vibrant grassroots movement that actively supported refugees and migrants.

The EU subsequently dealt with refugees and migrants as if they were a matter of security, rather than people displaced through wars, some of which were partly caused by EU countries, such as Britain and France. As authoritarian and right-wing political forces gathered strength, war navies began to patrol the Aegean and safe passage for refugees became nearly impossible, turning the Mediterranean into a killing field. In 2016 a deal was negotiated whereby all people 'irregularly' entering Greece would be returned to Turkey and given the option to apply for asylum. Turkey was to receive substantial sums to keep millions of refugees and migrants within its borders. That cynical deal trapped tens of thousands of people in Greece, often under atrocious conditions and without any prospect of moving to where they wished to go, or even being reunited with their families. The flows were staunched in 2017, but the problem was far from finally resolved as political and social instability continued in the Middle East and across North Africa.

The political and moral failure to deal with limited numbers of desperate people reflected the true state of the EU more accurately than acres of academic writing. There was no solidarity among member states, and EU law was honoured more in the breach than in the observance. The sovereignty of some countries was cynically by-passed, while that of others was reasserted according to national criteria. Fearful of the burgeoning right-wing reaction across the EU, country after country confronted the refugees by taking emergency measures, or simply turning a blind eye to them. After decades of neoliberalism and years of austerity, the EU could barely sustain even the forms of democracy in tackling the refugee crisis.

The impossibility of radical reform

Faced with this unforgiving reality, the first requirement for the Left is to tackle the belief that the EU could be radically reformed from within. This is a delusion that keeps reappearing despite the experience of the last two decades, and no-one expresses it more clearly than Yanis Varoufakis.

Following the SYRIZA débâcle, Varoufakis re-emerged at the head of a putative movement to 'democratize' the EU, called Democracy in Europe Movement 2025 (DiEM25). The founding document of DiEM25 makes the following three demands on the EU.[9] First, immediately establish full transparency in the workings of the key institutions. Second, within one year, return power to national parliaments on public debt, banking, investment, migration, and poverty. This would be achieved through the existing institutions of the EU via 'creative interpretation' of the Treaties and charters. Third, within two years, establish a Constitutional Assembly that would transform Europe into a 'full-fledged democracy with a sovereign Parliament respecting national self-determination and sharing power with national Parliaments, regional assemblies and municipal councils' by 2025, no less.

Perusing these statements, one is obliged to ask whether anything has been learnt from the disaster of SYRIZA. The answer appears to be no, since the demands are in essence the failed SYRIZA approach writ large. The lack of appreciation of the class and national nature of the EU is evident. DiEM25 might well produce a 'creative interpretation' of the Treaties of the EU, generating eloquent documents and intricate arguments, but it has absolutely no chance of also making it an effective interpretation.

The machinery of the EU, the tremendous weight of the *acquis*, and the authority of the ECJ ensure that the Treaties will continue to be interpreted in favour of advancing neoliberalism. Just as there is no normal politics within the EU, there is also no normal political contestation in determining the outlook of EU institutions. The EU is not a nation state over whose mechanisms the Left could give battle to shape their outlook and performance. It is a transnational juggernaut geared to neoliberal and hierarchical motion.

One simple example will suffice to establish this point. Decisions at the Council of the European Union – the body that makes the bulk of the laws, coordinates the actions of member states, and adopts the EU budget – are made through qualified majority voting.[10] This rule applies to about 80% of all EU legislation. Simply put, it requires that proposals are voted in by, first, 55% of member states (in practice, at least sixteen out of twenty-eight) and, second, member states representing at least 65% of the total EU population.[11] The notion that the proposals of DiEM25, imaginative as they would no doubt be, could ever command such majorities in an EU dominated by neoliberal ideology and German power does not bear contemplation. Class and national interests at the heart of the EU have completely solidified their institutional dominance. There is no way in for well-meaning reformers.

Of far greater consequence than DiEM25 are systemic reformers, such as Emmanuel Macron, President of France, for they also show the narrow limits of reforming the EU. The rise of Macron is itself a testament to the hollowing out of democracy in Europe. A politician who barely polled above 20% in the first round of the French elections in 2017 was hailed as the people's choice in favour of 'Europe'. There is nothing radical about Emmanuel Macron, an investment banker and minister of François Hollande, whose Socialist government followed the German lead throughout the Eurozone crisis. In electoral terms he was catapulted into the limelight as the French people rejected the established political system, leading to the collapse of the Socialist Party and the decline of the parties of the Right. More deeply, however, Macron's rise reflects the dead-end in which the French economy finds itself in the face of German ascendancy.

The French ruling strata made a historic miscalculation when they pushed for the EMU in the late 1980s and 1990s. In economic terms France, with its persistent competitiveness gap, weak current account, and steadily rising public debt, is not a match for Germany. It also has a heavily financialized economy affording a strong role to banks in determining economic policy. Advancing financialization has generated persistent pressures of unemployment, weak incomes, and diminished welfare provision. Society has been dispirited, class divisions have sharpened, and inequality has deepened.

Macron's elevation is a result of the peculiar class alignment in France in the 2010s. The French ruling bloc is aware of its diminished role in the EU, but is unwilling to exit the EMU, not least because of the domestic upheaval that would probably follow. Instead it hopes to defeat the domestic forces of labour with the intention of drawing competitive benefits and in the hope of thereby strengthening its position in the EU.

The working class and other plebeian layers, although they are deeply hostile to the political and social status quo, lack both clear alternatives and political leadership. Macron took advantage of the demise of the political status quo, drew on careful media manipulation, and attempted to offer a way out for the French establishment by proposing to reform the EU while also reforming France.

Macron's intentions with regard to the EU are based on the notion that the Franco-German axis, which dictated terms in the EU for decades but declined precipitously in the course of the Eurozone crisis, could be revived, thus opening up the prospect of wider reform. In a key speech made in September 2017 Macron presented a long list of suggested political and other reforms, including strengthening the monetary union by establishing a Finance Minister and a Eurozone budget.[12] His ideas appeared to chime with those of the European Commission, which in December that year also proposed reforms to strengthen the Eurozone, including appointing a European Finance Minister and allowing the ESM to intervene in the resolution of banking crises. Several months later, however, Macron's suggestions remained barely formulated notions, and that was far from accidental.

The Franco-German axis might be a cherished notion of the French ruling bloc, but in practice Germany has become the dominant force in the EU. Macron has basked in the political limelight only because of internal political disarray in Germany following elections in 2017 in which the Social Democrats effectively collapsed and a vocal right-wing movement emerged, making it hard to form a stable government. German society and politics are far from impervious to the effects of decades of relentless austerity coupled with the refugee crisis. German hegemony, after all, has fragile domestic foundations.

However, nothing will happen in the EU until Germany finally decides to act, and the German establishment will not allow changes that threaten its ability to generate external surpluses. Given the direction of development of the EU, Germany is likely to be tempted by forming variable groups of member states on the basis of specific economic characteristics and existing institutions. Formalizing peripheries and even developing combinations of core countries would be more amenable to conditional German hegemony than striving for greater integration of the EMU by creating new institutions. If the ESM was indeed reformed in this context, its role would probably be to enforce discipline across the union. In practice, when Germany is ready, a variant of the old debate between the 'economists' and the 'monetarists' will be played out once again, except that the 'economists' have already immeasurably strengthened their position. The result will probably be some form of compromise that will favour German industrial interests.

Macron's proposals to reform France, on the other hand, are the true voice of the French establishment seeking to defeat French labour. His approach sums up at once the wishes of the French ruling bloc and the historic impasse it faces. Labour 'reforms' are the wrong way for France to escape its subordinate position relative to Germany. Cutting labour costs would create recessionary pressures and increase social tensions, without substantially restoring French competitiveness within the EMU in view of the cumulative German advantage. By taking the path of Macron, the French establishment could perhaps inflict a defeat on French workers, but it would also compound the historical error it made almost three decades ago with the EMU.

A class-based stance for the Left

In this light the point of departure for a left strategy in Europe ought to be that the EU is neither a purveyor of 'soft power', nor a benevolent and humanitarian force. Rather, it is a hierarchical alliance of nation states that have created the institutional framework of a single market relentlessly promoting neoliberalism. The advantages offered to German capital by this dispensation are considerable. The advantages offered to other ruling blocs across Europe are more debatable and depend on particular circumstances.

There is no overarching capitalist class in Europe that has benefited from the EU, even if neoliberalism tends generally to favour capital against labour. And nor is there a European transnational historical bloc whose power sustains the further neoliberal evolution of the EU. Several historical blocs exist in Europe and relations among them are hegemonic, contested, and variable, while also being cooperative at critical junctures. The loss of sovereignty and the decline in democracy have been felt in very different ways across the continent.

The determining aspect of European political development remains class relations expressed primarily at the national level. These are naturally different for countries of the core compared to countries of the peripheries. The perception of the loss of sovereignty and decline of democracy, general as it is in Europe, varies among different countries, as does the underlying class reality. The search for sovereignty and the tribulations of democracy in Europe have reflected these varying class relations within the framework of the EU.

In 1848 Marx and Engels published *The Communist Manifesto*, famously claiming that 'A spectre is haunting Europe – the spectre of communism.'[13] They were ahead of the times, even if their book appeared on the cusp of the revolutions that swept the continent that year. What actually followed was Tsarist military repression in Hungary in 1849, the dictatorship of Louis Napoleon Bonaparte in France in 1851, and the rise of Bismarck in Prussia in the 1860s. It took more than two decades for Marx and Engels' far-sightedness to become apparent with the Paris Commune of 1871.

The spectre of communism does not haunt today's Europe, but the spirit of discontent is certainly abroad, feeding on the demands for democracy and sovereignty. There is a great risk of an authoritarian tide engulfing the continent. It is instructive, therefore, to be reminded of the following passages from *The Communist Manifesto*:

> The working men have no country. We cannot take from them what they have not got. Since the proletariat must first of all acquire political supremacy, must rise to be the leading class of the nation, must constitute itself the nation, it is so far, itself national, though not in the bourgeois sense of the word.
>
> National differences and antagonism between peoples are daily more and more vanishing, owing to the

development of the bourgeoisie, to freedom of commerce, to the world market, to uniformity in the mode of production and in the conditions of life corresponding thereto.

The supremacy of the proletariat will cause them to vanish still faster. United action, of the leading civilised countries at least, is one of the first conditions for the emancipation of the proletariat.[14]

The European Left would do well to revisit these ideas if it is to develop a coherent attitude toward the EU. For Marx and Engels, the working class is 'national' despite workers having 'no country' and aiming to eliminate national differences. There is no contradiction in this statement. The internationalism of capital is about competition and profit leading to national antagonisms, while that of labour is about solidarity and united action. The 'nation' has a very different meaning for the two classes.

Since the signing of the Treaty of Maastricht the class relations that underpin the European project have become steadily transparent. On the one hand, the plebeian layers, which were never in thrall to 'Europeanism' and have never accepted the notion that nation states should surrender sovereignty to a transnational entity, have become more hostile and rejectionist toward European institutions. After all, there has never been a mass movement of workers in favour of the EU or the EEC, but at most a sullen acceptance. On the other, the privileged layers, including broad sections of the professional middle class with access to the media, the universities, research institutes, and so on, have become closely attached to the notion that the EU stands for progress.

The 'depoliticization' of the economy, the hollowing out of democracy, and the loss of popular sovereignty are acutely felt by workers and the poor in Europe. Caught in the maelstrom of 2007–9 and the Eurozone turmoil, they have experienced austerity and a host of social problems related to unemployment, wages, housing, and welfare provision. In the past the Left would have explained the powerlessness of plebeian Europe in terms of the fundamental relations of capitalism and the power of capital. It would have rejected the false notion that the problems of everyday life are due to impoverished migrants and displaced refugees. It would have called for socialism and challenged directly the EMU and the EU.

Instead much of the European Left has developed its own illusions about the EU by embellishing mainstream perceptions with notions of democracy, egalitarianism, and, not least, social liberalism, including racial equality, sexual equality, and so on. Several left-wing parties perceive of the EU, and even the EMU, as inherently progressive historical developments that have overcome the nation state and ought to be defended.[15] The strongest adherents of these ideas are the social democrats, but the impact is widely felt across the Left.

Therein lies the problem with the Left in Europe today. Its attachment to the EU as an inherently progressive development prevents it from being radical, and indeed integrates it into the neoliberal structures of European capitalism. The Left has become increasingly cut off from its historic constituency, the workers and the poor of Europe, who have naturally sought a political voice elsewhere. The result has been politically catastrophic, especially for the social democrats, who are rightly perceived as staunch defenders of the status quo. Inevitably the vacuum created by the Left has been steadily filled by some of the worst political forces in European history, including the extreme Right.

For the plebeian classes of Europe, sovereignty has never been anathema. On the contrary, it is understood as the power to make and apply laws, to design and implement social and economic policy, and to elect and hold to account those who administer those laws and policies. For workers and the poor, sovereignty has a popular dimension representing the right to be consulted but also to refuse government policies. Popular sovereignty goes directly against the fetishism of the economy as a technocratic entity, while also protecting a cultural and political community from the will of another.

Popular sovereignty and democracy are dangerous for the ruling elites of capitalist societies because, as far as the plebeian layers are concerned, they are closely interwoven with each other. To establish popular sovereignty and democracy, working people must necessarily contest the national levers of power – communal mechanisms, the institutions of local authority, the local and national electoral process, the mass media, the executive machinery of the state, and so on. By contesting power across a range of national institutions, workers would be seeking the position of a ruling social class that could shape the outlook of the country in opposition to the ruling capitalist bloc. They would be striving to constitute the 'nation'. That is the basis on which to develop a strategy for the Left in Europe today.

What is the Left to do?

What, then, is the European Left to do? The lesson of SYRIZA is paramount in this regard. If the Left intends to implement radical anti-capitalist policies and effectively to confront the neoliberal juggernaut of the EU, it must be prepared for a rupture. There has to be a break, an upheaval, an overturning of prevailing conditions, for things to change in Europe. There must be a rupture with the domestic power structures that have a vested interest in the current arrangements. There must also be a rupture with the transnational institutions of the EU that sustain the current arrangements.

A crucial step in this direction would be rejection of the EMU. The monetary union is the backbone of the single market, and the most effective disciplining device for the imposition of neoliberal policy and ideology. The nations of Europe do not need a common currency to engage in free and fruitful interaction with each other, and they certainly do not need the euro. Conversely, the longer the EMU perseveres and the more rigid it becomes, the more difficult it would be to implement anti-capitalist policies in Europe.

For the peripheral nations, and especially for the Southern periphery, exiting the EMU is imperative. Getting out of the iron trap is the way to adopt policies that could expand the economy, absorb unemployment through the creation of well-paid jobs, reduce poverty, and place countries on the path of sustained growth. Exit is certainly not an easy process, but by now there is considerable knowledge on how it could be achieved with

131

as little disruption as possible.[16] If it were consensual, the costs would be further reduced.

For the core countries the issue of the EMU is considerably more complex, since it involves altogether dismantling the monetary union and putting alternative arrangements in its place. The EMU should certainly not be replaced by unfettered competition in the foreign exchange markets. Europe requires a system of stabilizing exchange rates coupled with a means of making payments among countries. The technical knowledge to achieve these aims exists, and even some of the mechanisms of the old European Monetary System are still extant. The system failed in the early 1990s for reasons already explained in Chapter 2, but the underlying notion of stabilizing exchange rates was valid.

The EU is a huge economic entity in which most trade takes place among member states. In such an economy it is certainly feasible to stabilize exchange rates and produce far better economic results than the euro has done over the two decades of its existence. For that it would be necessary to have a proper anchor country as well as to apply controls on the movement of capital across Europe. Flexibility could then return to rebalancing the external relations of EU economies. With capital controls in place it would even be plausible to devise a new joint means of payment based on principles of solidarity that would be used among European states only to facilitate international transactions and not as domestic currency.

Dismantling the EMU would create room for broader radical change in the EU. After all, it would mean drastically altering the character of the ECB, the Eurogroup, the Eurogroup Working Group, and the ESM. It would remove the external constraints on the operations of other EU institutions, including the policing of the fiscal activities of member states. It would loosen the grip of the *acquis* by removing a host of directives and regulations. It would also remove the harshest disciplining device on labour across much of Europe. Dismantling the EMU would be a decisive blow against the neoliberal regime of the EU.

For broader radical reforms of the EU to take place, however, and for the dismantling of the EMU to make full sense, there would also have to be domestic programmes that directly challenged the power of capital. Each country would have to tailor its own programme according to its needs, but key elements would be in common. In the short term they would include, first, lifting austerity and, second, engaging in income and wealth redistribution.

It is imperative that austerity is lifted. Fiscal and monetary policy ought to be deployed to boost domestic demand with the aim of reducing unemployment and raising incomes. In a huge economy such as the EU, the sources of demand ought to be sought domestically in the first instance. This holds for countries of the core and for those in the peripheries, but also for the hegemonic power. Germany ought to wean itself from its destructive neo-mercantilism by focusing on its domestic economy.

Boosting domestic demand would necessarily include redistributing income and wealth away from capital and toward labour. Inequality has to be tackled as a matter of urgency across Europe, in both core and periphery. It makes economic sense in several EU countries to raise wages as a means of supporting aggregate demand.[17]

It also makes economic sense to raise the tax burden on the corporations and the rich, including on wealth. Restoring labour rights and protecting employment as well as re-strengthening the welfare state through provision for health, housing, and education would be integral steps toward reducing inequality. There is nothing infeasible about such policies in contemporary Europe. It is entirely a matter of political and social choices that reflect the balance of power between labour and capital.

In the medium and long term, however, far more complex issues would arise for any left programme. Growth has to be strengthened and European economies have to be reshaped. Globalization has proceeded apace during the last four decades by expanding supply chains across the world and boosting trade, much of it within these chains. The global balance of manufacturing and trade has dramatically changed with the emergence of China as a major industrial power. Ecological destruction has escalated as globalization has spread its tentacles across the world. Financialization has also proceeded apace, leading to proportionate overexpansion of the financial sector, the counterpart of which has been weak investment by productive enterprises in mature countries. These profound economic changes, moreover, have coincided with a widespread revolution in telecommunications and information technology.

Yet the introduction of new technology has failed to raise the productivity of labour with a similar vigour to other technological revolutions in the history of capitalism.[18] Weak productivity growth will prove a major problem in devising growth policies for Europe in the future. At the same time the new technology has vastly increased the availability of information about economic agents, even down to the level of individual activities and preferences. An era of Big Data appears to be dawning that will transform the operations of commercial capital, industrial capital, and, above all, banking capital. The growing power of capital over economic and social life that this affords raises profound questions of individual freedom and rights. Crucially, it has also given a tremendous boost to the feasibility of rational economic planning.

Against this background the Left in Europe ought to propose industrial policy tailored to the needs of individual countries with two characteristics in common. First, banks should be placed under public ownership and control to begin to reverse financialization, and to provide for the investment needs of enterprises and the consumption needs of households. Public investment banks adapted to the peculiarities of particular countries would be vital levers to generate an investment wave in Europe. Not least, public banks would facilitate control and regulation over the private banking sector, which are essential prerequisites for a radical growth policy.

Second, public investment in and public ownership of key resources should be given pride of place. They are necessary to renew the infrastructure of Europe, including housing, to mobilize new technologies and Big Data in ways that protect democratic rights and the public interest, and to support innovation and the growth of productivity. Public investment could also support the revival of private investment in Europe – especially if profit making through financial assets was drastically curtailed – thus helping to bridge the gap between core and peripheries. Last but not least, public investment and public property could provide the foundations for environmentally aware growth that aimed to protect the natural world.

Elements of this approach in the context of Greece characterized the left wing of SYRIZA, and at times it was called 'Left Keynesianism'. Whenever the term was meant as abuse, it merely showed a lack of understanding of how class struggle unfolds in practice. These policies would tilt the balance of power against capital and in favour of labour, thus preparing the ground for the socialist transformation of Europe. Needless to say, it would take much more to achieve socialism, including a profound change of property relations favouring public against private property. But the immediate aim for the Left would be to challenge the entrenched class interests that have brought Europe to its present pass. If the Left went down the path outlined above, it could expect fierce opposition.

Hostility should first be expected from the domestic mechanisms of power whose interests would be directly threatened. Hostility should also be expected from the mechanisms of the EU, since an industrial policy based on public ownership and a range of economic controls would run directly counter to the logic of the single market. The neoliberal machine in Brussels would not tolerate a challenge to the institutional organization of the EU and to the power of the *acquis communautaire*. The prospect of exiting the EU would inevitably arise.

The crucial point to observe with regard to EU exit is that the broader reshaping of the world economy during the last four decades, including the rise of new technologies, the spread of supply chains, the growth of trade, and the rise of China, has not required conditions similar to the European single market to take place. Indeed, in historical terms, the dynamic emergence and growth of capitalism has never occurred according to neoliberal precepts and textbooks. Moreover, the great crisis of 2007–9 marked the high point of neoliberal ascendancy and destroyed the verities of the preceding decades. The future path of official policy is likely to include elements of protection and control over markets. In short, the ideology of the single market is already redolent of an older era. The internationalization of production and the spread of trade do not require a single market. By the same token, exiting or abolishing the single market is not tantamount to establishing a regime of autarky behind national borders.

Faced with EU hostility, therefore, the Left should reject the single market and its institutional and legal framework. It should argue in favour of controls on the movement of goods, services, capital, and people, in the absence of which it would be impossible to apply a radical programme in the direction of socialism. It should also reject the authority of the *acquis* and the ECJ, thus beginning to disentangle national from community legislation and re-establishing the pre-eminence of national jurisdiction. Ultimately there is no other way to recoup popular and national sovereignty. If this implies being presented with an ultimatum to exit the EU, so be it.

Valuable insight into this issue can be gained from the travails of Brexit. Britain is a historic centre of capitalist accumulation and a leading world power which wisely refused to join the EMU and on this score alone cannot be considered as a core country of the EU, in spite of its evident weight in European economics and politics. The decision to exit the EU, taken via a referendum in the

137

summer of 2016, showed that the EU is reversible. The negotiations that have followed have cast light on what it means to exit the union.

The British historical bloc, an alliance of financiers, merchants, industrialists, and the professional upper middle class, has been profoundly split on the question of Europe for decades. The core sections have unquestionably been in favour of EU membership, and some have even been in support of joining the monetary union. But there have also been strong elements in favour of exiting the EU and keeping away from the EMU. The interests behind these components of the British historical bloc are not clearly demarcated, and their differences are not purely economic. Equally important in explaining the split is sovereignty and its associated ideology.

The evolution of the EU and its predecessor, the EEC, during the last four decades and the emergence of rigid institutional mechanisms that have restricted the sovereignty of member states have had a pronounced effect on Britain. Loss of sovereignty has been the prism refracting the long-standing split of the British historical bloc with regard to the EU. In so doing it has created a political split within the Conservative Party, which actually took Britain into the EEC in 1973 and is the traditional voice of the British establishment. The focal points of contestation have been who makes and applies the laws, and who takes decisions on immigration. Crucially, the split has allowed the muted popular discontent with neoliberal policies over the last four decades to find a voice, thus swinging the vote in the referendum of 2016 in favour of exit.

The British referendum was one of those rare historical moments when a rift within the ruling layers allows a deeper rift in society to manifest itself. British society is split between a minority that has benefited from neo-liberal policies, and the large majority that has borne the brunt of the concomitant transformation of British capitalism in recent decades. There is no doubt that the working class and the plebeian strata have generally tended to support Brexit.[19] The vote to Leave became a vote against the dominant wing of the British histori-cal bloc, which had clearly expressed its preference for Remain. It was a vote by proxy against austerity, poor jobs, and the decline in welfare provision, particularly since the great crisis of 2007–9. Moreover, far from rep-resenting a surrender to racism, rabid nationalism, and right-wing authoritarianism, the referendum facilitated the radicalization of British politics in an unexpected way. The Conservative Party barely won the general election of 2017, and the real victor was a revived Labour Party, with a manifesto based on a social demo-cratic programme opposing austerity and even calling for nationalization of the railways and other resources.

The period following the election in which the nego-tiations with the EU have unfolded has been instructive concerning the reality of exit even for a powerful European country such as Britain. The EU has assumed an implacable attitude, particularly with regard to the power of the ECJ and the primacy of the *acquis commu-nautaire*. It has insisted that, if British capital is to have the advantages of the single market, it must accept the jurisdiction of ECJ and the Four Freedoms. Deep disar-ray has emerged in the Conservative Party, reflecting the inherent difficulty of the choice facing the British histor-ical bloc. For, as EU insistence has made clear, if Britain is to recapture its sovereignty, it cannot remain in the single market. Consequently, the country must seek a different trade relationship with the EU and the rest of the world. But from the perspective of British capital, and especially of the financial sector based in the City of London, there is no trade arrangement that is superior to the neoliberal framework provided by the EU. The choice for the Conservative Party and the British historical bloc is harsh.

An answer for Britain – and a pointer for the rest of Europe – could be provided by the Labour Party. The single market is hardly compatible with the aim of beating neoliberalism, restructuring the British economy, and reducing the power of the City in favour of workers and the poor through a far-reaching industrial strategy. It is open to the Labour Party to provide a fresh choice for Britain by opting out of the single market while applying a radical growth programme to overturn neoliberalism. On this basis Britain could strike new trade agreements to protect output and employment, without complying with the Four Freedoms of the single market.

It is almost redundant to repeat in this light that exiting the EU would not necessarily be a nationalist step, and nor would it represent a return to competing and warring states in Europe. On the contrary, it could signal the emergence of a radical internationalism that would draw on domestic strength and reject the dysfunctional and hegemonic structures of the EU. It could enable concrete economic policies creating a true basis for solidarity in Europe, and giving fresh content to popular sovereignty and democratic rights. It could also lead to new forms of interstate alliances in Europe that would reflect the altered balance of domestic class forces.

140

These would be the grounds on which to demonstrate in practice that Hayek, though presciently analysing the direction of travel of a federal union of capitalist states, was wide of the mark when he claimed that a federal union in Europe would necessarily promote 'liberalism'. The actual form and content of renewed European interaction would depend on the internal social and political regime of member states. Workers' internationalism always starts at home. If capitalism was challenged domestically, several forms of socialist federal integration would become possible in Europe. That is a feasible and worthwhile aim for the European Left. The sooner it begins to engage in open debate and to act along these lines, the better for the people of the continent.

Notes

Chapter 1 The European Union and the Left

1 The text of the Single European Act is available at *http://eur-lex.europa.eu/legal-content/EN/TXT/?uri= LEGISSUM%3Axy0027*. The text of the Maastricht Treaty is available at *http://eur-lex.europa.eu/legal-con tent/EN/TXT/PDF/?uri=OJ:C:1992:191:FULL&from =EN*.
2 See Fukuyama (1992).
3 This is fully appreciated in the academic literature, which recognizes the end of the 'permissive consensus' after Maastricht, that is, the end of a period in which European integration proceeded mostly from above as a project operated by the elites of European countries. After Maastricht, 'Europe' became an issue of national and popular politics and the functioning of the EU acquired new characteristics. See Hooghe and Marks (2009) and Bickerton, Hodson, and Puetter (2015).
4 More than a decade after publishing *The End of History and the Last Man*, Fukuyama (2007) helpfully explained in the British *Guardian* that his model for the triumph of 'post-historical' liberal democracy was not the USA

but the EU precisely because it was transnational (Fukuyama 2007).

5 Academics have long discussed the 'crisis of representation' in Europe: see, for instance, the special issues of *West European Politics* (Hayward 1995) and the *European Journal of Political Research* (summed up in Norris 1997). The absence of a *demos* in Europe and the shifting boundaries of power between the EU and nation states are acknowledged to hamper democratic practice and discourse (see Weiler, Haltern, and Mayer 1995).

6 Even ardent supporters of the EU have acknowledged that much of the blame lies with liberal democracy itself (see Zielonka 2018).

7 See Callinicos (2015). See also Bugaric (2013), who discusses the major constraints imposed by the EU on left politics.

8 For the context of the Mitterrand government and its importance in eventually setting up the Economic and Monetary Union, see James (2012: chs 5–6).

9 See Negri (2005).

10 This section draws heavily on Lapavitsas (2017).

11 For a still useful summary of the main features of neoliberalism, see Saad-Filho and Johnston (2005).

12 The literature is large, particularly in the field of International Relations. For a recent survey of competing approaches, see Webber (2014).

13 Examples are legion. Note, for instance, the speech by Martin Schulz, then the leader of the German Social Democratic Party, at the Party conference in December 2017, calling for a United States of Europe by 2025, which would fight austerity and promote investment across Europe. Indeed, Schulz proposed that countries not prepared to agree to his version of 'More Europe' should be excluded from the union altogether (see Buck and Chazan 2017).

Chapter 2 The Evolution of the EU: From Maastricht to Now

1 Milward (1994) powerfully documents the recovery of the nation state in Europe during those decades, claiming that it proved a pillar of the EEC, while also gaining strength and legitimacy from the drive toward European integration. From this perspective, there is no simple opposition between national and transnational institutions in Europe.

2 Hayek's 1939 essay is not as widely referenced as it should be in the enormous literature on the EU and EEC. It has, however, been systematically read by critical voices on the Left. Thus, Bonefeld (1998 and 2001) was one of the first to pay attention to it. See also Gowan (2009), Anderson (2010), and Streeck (2014) for extensive discussion.

3 See Hayek (1939: 258–61).

4 See Hayek (1939: 261–4).

5 See Hayek (1939: 263).

6 See Hayek (1939: 266).

7 See Hayek (1939: 268–9).

8 See Hayek (1939: 271).

9 See Hayek (1939: 255–7).

10 For a penetrating analysis of this point, especially the contrast between neoliberal and social democratic views on federation in Europe, see Reho (2017).

11 The disciplinary core of the theories of regional integration in the EU is quite mixed. The historian Alan Milward (1994) put forth a cogent case for the dominant role of the nation state in European integration and the benefits drawn by member states from pooling sovereignty. The political theorist Andrew Moravscik (1991, 1993, and mostly 1998) postulated the theory of 'liberal intergovernmentalism' based on the notion that nation states are the driving force in the EU, but that they have to

bargain with other states to impose their preferences. For Moravscik, the EU can be expected to march on steadily. A still useful review of this literature is provided by Marks, Hooghe, and Blank (1996).

12 The disciplinary core of this current is also mixed, but it relies heavily on the descriptive accounts of the relationship between societies and institutions by the political theorist Ernst Haas (1958, 1975). For Haas, especially in his early writings, European integration proceeded as cooperation in some fields generated spill-overs inducing cooperation in others, while also creating transnational institutions with a stake in further integration. See also Caporaso and Keeler (1995) and Caporaso (1998).

13 See Höpner and Schäfer (2012).

14 See Lapavitsas (2013: ch. 4).

15 As Polanyi (1944) showed decades ago.

16 See Hayek (1976: 23–4).

17 The text of the report is available at *http://aei.pitt. edu/1002/1/monetary_werner_final.pdf*.

18 See Torres (2007) for a clear and brief discussion.

19 See Torres (2007).

20 For further analysis of these issues, see Flassbeck and Lapavitsas (2015).

21 The text of the report is available at *http://ec.europa.eu/ economy_finance/publications/pages/publication6161_ en.pdf*.

22 See Dyson (1994 and 2000) for the political influence of 'Sound Money' in setting up the Eurozone. See also Marcussen (1999).

23 See Wyplosz (2006). It is worth remarking that Wyplosz wrote a lengthy and complex account of the 'dark sides' of the EMU without even mentioning the trajectory of wages in member countries.

24 Verdun (1999) documented the extraordinary influence of central bankers in the Delors Committee determining

the main parameters of EMU. James (2012: ch. 8) has also shown the pivotal role of the Committee of Central Bankers, established in 1964, in setting up the EMU. There is an unbroken line of continuity between the staff of the Committee and the European Central Bank.

25 See Wyplosz (2006: 230).

26 See Baun (1995–6: 623); see also Heise (2005) for an early view of a 'Germanic Europe' likely to emerge from the EMU. Eichengreen (1993) also believes that the EMU was not economically necessary but politically expedient.

27 It is almost superfluous to mention that the EMU does not meet the putative requirements of an 'Optimum Currency Area' (OCA) set out by Mundell (1961). Most notably the mobility of labour among member states is in practice hindered by a host of cultural and institutional factors. But the notion of the euro having 'architectural flaws' is far wider than whether it meets the conditions of the OCA. Indeed, it is debatable whether the OCA conditions have any true content at all. A well-functioning monetary union is possible in their absence (see Flassbeck and Lapavitsas 2015).

28 Conservative Anglo-Saxon economists had made this point already in the 1990s (see, e.g., Feldstein 1997; and 'An interview with Milton Friedman. Interviewed by John B. Taylor, May 2000', in Samuelson and Barnett 2007: ch. 6). See also Pisany-Ferry (2011) and, more recently, Stiglitz (2016).

29 See Boonstra (2010) and Delpla and von Weizsäcker (2010).

30 For the institutional details of European central banking after Maastricht, see Smits (1996).

31 The Maastricht Criteria were subjected to sustained academic criticism as soon as the Treaty was completed. Buiter, Corsetti, and Frankel (1993), for instance, decried their deflationary nature.

32 For the exact wording see *http://www.lisbon-treaty.org/ wcm/the-lisbon-treaty/treaty-on-the-functioning-of-the- european-union-and-comments/part-3-union-policies- and-internal-actions/title-viii-economic-and-monetary- policy/chapter-1-economic-policy/393-article-125.html*.

33 The conditional nature of German hegemony in Europe has for many years been a source of debate among political scientists, with many denying its existence (see, e.g., McNamara and Jones 1996). The role of Germany in the Eurozone crisis ought to help settle that debate.

34 See Marx (1867: 240–4).

35 For further analysis of financialization from this perspective, see Lapavitsas (2013).

Chapter 3 The Ascendancy of Germany and the Division of Europe

1 For an excellent and concise historical account of the rise of German hegemony in the EU, see Hadjiiossif (2017).

2 See Lapavitsas and Powell (2013), who also note the strong turn of France toward financialization during the last four decades.

3 See Lapavitsas (2013: ch. 8) for the peculiarities of German financialization in view especially of the country's tradition of bank-based finance. See also Stockhammer (2009), who considers Germany an instance of export-led financialization.

4 See Höpner and Lutter (2014).

5 See Lapavitsas (2013: ch. 8).

6 See Höpner and Lutter (2014).

7 Historically, German capital has been closely connected to Central and Eastern Europe, and there are deeply rooted cultural and other links among these countries that have facilitated the flows of foreign direct investment and the construction of supply chains (see Gross 2013).

8 For further analysis of internal developments in Germany and their importance to the neoliberal transformation of the EU, see Scharpf (2010, 2016), Höpner (2014), and Streeck (2016). See also Flassbeck and Lapavitsas (2015).

9 For the decline in union power in Germany, see Yamamura and Streeck (2003).

10 See Bonefeld (2012, 2017); see also Blyth (2013: 135–7). Bulmer (2014) argues that domestic ordoliberalism in Germany has undermined its ability to act as the hegemon of Europe, but the reverse is more likely the case.

11 See Hien and Joerges (2018) for an outstanding account of the specific character of ordoliberalism from a legal perspective as well as its retreat in Germany.

12 Ruoff (2016) shows the rapid rise of precarious work and the decline of stable employment after the Hartz Reforms. The rapid increase in low-paid employment already from the mid-1990s is noted by Hassel (2014). Benassi and Dorigatti (2015) document the relentless rise of agency work at the heart of the German industrial complex, eliciting the response of IG Metall. Posted work in the construction sector (i.e. work undertaken by employees sent by their employers to another EU member state) has also grown enormously (see Wagner 2015). The figures can be striking: thus Bispinck and Schulten (2011), drawing on the German Federal Employment Agency, report that 'as a rule of thumb' 40% of the total labour force can be considered as having an 'atypical' employment relationship.

13 The emergence of a dual labour market in Germany (i.e. the split between workers in relative stable employment and workers in precarious and temporary employment) is well attested (see, e.g., Hassell 2014). The 'flexibility' generated by precarious employment has contributed to lower unemployment in Germany after the global crisis of 2007–9, which is often referred to as the 'German Labour Market Miracle' (see Burda and Hunt 2011; Caliendo

and Hogenacker 2012). This 'miracle' was achieved at the price of worse living conditions for the bulk of wage labour.

14 See Di Carlo (2018).

15 See Lapavitsas (2013: ch. 7).

16 See, for instance, European Commission (2011, section II).

17 Considerable confusion surrounds the role of national competitiveness in the Eurozone crisis. The Commission's approach is certainly misleading, but that should not imply denigrating the importance of national competitiveness in explaining the crisis. For an instance of this misunderstanding, see Storm and Naastepad (2015).

18 See Flassbeck and Lapavitsas (2015).

19 Similar results obtain for productivity per hour worked rather than person.

20 See Lapavitsas et al. (2010b).

21 The net international investment position measures the stock of international assets held by agents of a national economy minus the stock of domestic assets held by foreign agents.

22 For the purposes of this chapter, the core of the EU is assumed to comprise Germany, France, and Italy. If the Netherlands, Austria, and other countries were included, the analysis would have been much more complicated without commensurate benefit.

23 Path-breaking empirical work along these lines has been systematically undertaken at the Vienna Institute for International Economic Studies (see, e.g., Landesmann and Hanzl-Weiss 2013; Landesmann and Leitner [with Stehrer] 2015; Hanzl-Weiss and Landesmann 2016).

24 German FDI in France and Italy (but also Britain) has been either stagnant or falling, and is much less important than in the three core countries shown in Figure 10. Moreover, Asia, including China, has absorbed a modest volume of German FDI, similar to Britain.

25 The International Monetary Fund has been aware of some of these developments for some time now (see its extensive report in International Monetary Fund 2013).

Chapter 4 The Eurozone Crisis: Class Interests and Hegemonic Power

1 See Lapavitsas (2013: ch. 9).
2 Ireland also found itself in deep crisis in 2010, and the country certainly moves in a peripheral orbit within the EMU. But its economy is distinctly different to that of Southern peripheral countries since it acts as a tax haven for a host of US multinationals operating in Europe and elsewhere. The crisis in Ireland, nonetheless, shared several common features with other EMU countries, notably the tremendous expansion of domestic debt which eventually fell on the shoulders of the public. For that reason reference will be made to Ireland throughout the subsequent chapters.
3 Analysis in this section draws on Lapavitsas (2018). There is an extensive mainstream literature on balance of payments crises of the 'sudden stop' variety (see Calvo, Izquierdo, and Talvi 2006 and Calvo 2007; see also Merler and Pisany-Ferry 2012 and Baldwin and Giavazzi 2015).
4 See Lapavitsas et al. (2010a).
5 See the extraordinary letter of Jean-Claude Trichet, the President of the ECB, and Miguel Fernández Ordóñez, Governor of the Bank of Spain, to José Luis Rodríguez Zapatero, Prime Minister of Spain, on 5 August 2011, available at *https://www.ecb.europa.eu/pub/pdf/other/ 2011-08-05-letter-from-trichet-and-fernandez-ordonez- to-zapateroen.pdf*. See also the even more extraordinary letter by Mr Trichet and Mario Draghi, his successor as President of the ECB, to Silvio Berlusconi, the Prime

Minister of Italy, written on the same day, available at *http://www.voltairenet.org/article171574.html*.

6 For a relatively old but still useful account see Fine, Lapavitsas, and Pincus (2001).

7 This section draws on Lapavitsas, Mariolis, and Gavrielidis (2017). For lengthy institutional detail on the policies of the EU since the crisis, see Tsipouri (2015). For a brief summary of the policies and related reforms, see Ioannou, Leblond, and Niemann (2015).

8 For a succinct account of the role of the ECB in the early period of the crisis, see Darvas and Merler (2013).

9 See International Monetary Fund (2016).

10 See Tuori (2016).

11 The provision of bail-out funds and the creation of the ESM posed a challenge to Article 125 of the Lisbon Treaty, the so-called 'no bail-out' clause. In a remarkable example of the law bending to the force of circumstances, the European Court of Justice found in 2012 (the Pringle case) that establishing the ESM does not contradict Article 125 because the granting of loans is only an indirect assumption of responsibility for the actions of another state. Formally this is, of course, true, but the blurring of the lines is undeniable (see *https://eur-lex.europa.eu/legal-content/EN/TXT/?uri=CELEX:62012CP0370*).

12 See Argyroulis (2017) for an incisive account of how the Greek crisis was used as a lever for the hardening of the EMU's fiscal stance.

13 See Lapavitsas et al. (2012).

14 Note that after Mario Draghi, the President of the ECB, declared that he would do 'whatever it takes' to rescue the euro in 2012, very little actually changed in terms of ECB credit creation. For a verbatim account of his speech, see *https://www.ecb.europa.eu/press/key/date/2012/html/sp120726.en.html*.

Chapter 5 Greece in the Iron Trap of the Euro

1 This chapter and the next draw heavily on Lapavitsas (2018).
2 As was noted even by De Grauwe (2011). Only a few voices at the time pointed to the general nature of the Eurozone crisis, and these typically came from outside the economics mainstream. See, for instance, Lapavitsas et al. (2010a), which subsequently appeared in Lapavitsas et al. (2012). For further analysis along similarly heterodox lines, see also Cesaratto and Stirati (2010) and Scharpf (2011).
3 See Lapavitsas et al. (2010a).
4 For a clear example that focuses on Greek export performance, see Böwer, Michou, and Ungerer (2014). But see also Sinn (2014), who makes a similar point without agreeing with Commission policy.
5 See Nikiforos, Papadimitriou, and Zezza (2016) for the path of real effective exchange rates in Greece.
6 The following paragraphs draw on Katsinos and Mariolis (2012), Mariolis (2013, 2016), and Lapavitsas, Mariolis, and Gavrielidis (2017).
7 Aliber (2010) was one of the first to stress the importance of the structural shift in the Greek economy together with the deleterious impact of capital flows and the euro.
8 See Vavouras (2013).
9 See Mariolis (2016); see also Lapavitsas et al. (2010b), which subsequently appeared in Lapavitsas et al. (2012). Greek saving is further analysed by Katsimi and Moutos (2010).
10 See Lapavitsas et al. (2010a).
11 See Lapavitsas et al. (2010a).
12 See Gourinchas, Philippon, and Vayanos (2016).
13 See Lapavitsas et al. (2010a).
14 All figures on Greek debt come from Lapavitsas et al. (2010b), one of the earliest decompositions of Greek debt following the outbreak of the crisis.

15 On this point see also Gourinchas, Philippon, and Vayanos (2016).

16 See Artavanis, Morse, and Tsoutsoura (2012), who estimate that in 2009 alone there were at least 28 billion euros of unreported income by self-employed professionals, a tremendous sum by Greek standards.

17 As was pointed out by Buchheit and Gulati (2010) in one of the earliest and most penetrating analyses of Greek public debt.

18 For a meticulous account of the series of events and policies, see Kyriakidis (2016).

19 TARGET-2 is a system of interbank settlements operated by the Eurosystem and the ECB. It allows the National Central Banks that comprise the Eurosystem to make payments to each other by registering debits. As that happens, other central banks would obviously be accumulating credits. In effect, one central bank would be lending to another as payments are made. Since the outbreak of the Eurozone crisis the biggest creditor has been the Bundesbank and the biggest debtors, in order, have been the central banks of Italy, Spain, and Greece. The accumulation of TARGET-2 debts reflects the economic weakness of the Southern periphery as well as of Italy within the EMU.

20 See also Pisani-Ferry, Sapir, and Wolff (2013).

21 For the likely implications of devaluation for the Greek economy, see Katsinos and Mariolis (2012), one of the few careful empirical studies of the issue.

22 For the likely impact on fiscal space of various measures to restructure Greek public debt, see Lapavitsas and Munevar (2014).

23 See International Monetary Fund (2016).

24 It has been estimated that out of the funds provided to Greece by the first and the second bail-outs, only 4.5% have actually gone to financing primary deficits. The rest

have covered the needs of servicing the public debt, that is, protecting the interests of foreign lenders in the first instance (see Rocholl and Stahmer 2016).

25 See Blanchard and Leigh (2013).

26 See Greek Public Debt Management Agency, available at *http://www.pdma.gr/index.php/en/*.

27 See Zettelmeyer, Trebesch, and Gulati (2013).

28 Wyplosz and Sgherri (2016: 41) have called it 'the most dramatic credit migration from private into official hands in the history of sovereign debt'. It was not a 'migration' that benefited the Greek people.

29 See Flassbeck and Lapavitsas (2013, 2015).

30 This is one of the most striking aspects of the Fund's internal review (see International Monetary Fund 2016).

31 See International Monetary Fund (2016: 31).

32 For a penetrating discussion of Gramsci's concept and its usefulness in analysing the Eurozone crisis, see Sotiris (2018).

33 The predatory attitude of the Greek state toward society and its role in sustaining the power of the changing 'historical bloc' since independence in 1830 was discussed by Kostis (2015), though certainly not in the terms, or from the standpoint, of this book.

34 For further discussion of the broader social role of money, see Lapavitsas (2013).

35 Greece appears to be similar to Italy in this respect. The ideological role of the euro in Italy, particularly its association with progress, modernity, efficiency, and overcoming various putative national weaknesses, was extensively documented by Giurlando (2016).

36 Exceptions, especially among economists, were remarkably few. Prominent among these were Mariolis (e.g. 2016) and Skaperdas (2011).

37 The leadership of the Left Platform fell on Panayotis Lafazanis. For evidence that the dead-end of Tsipras's

strategy was clearly understood, see Flassbeck and Lapavitsas (2015) on the likely outcome of the 'tough negotiations'. That book was published a day before SYRIZA won the January election in 2015.

38 The self-serving and unreliable account of events in Varoufakis (2017) indirectly confirms this view. A politically sharper – and considerably shorter – account of the SYRIZA defeat is by Sheehan (2017), even though she was an outsider to events.

39 The description of that first Eurogroup meeting in Varoufakis (2017: 220–304) runs to eighty-four pages. This lengthy account effectively seeks to mask the complete failure of the strategy.

Chapter 6 Seeking Democracy, Sovereignty, and Socialism

1 See Scharpf (2006, 2011) on the 'democratic deficit' of the EU and its ominous implications for labour conditions and workers' rights. See also Weiler (2012) for an account of the political deficit in the EU, that is, the lack of democracy because of a lack of politics in EU institutions. Weiler also stresses the importance of 'messianism' for EU legitimacy, that is, the notion that 'Europe' is good in itself (see also Mair and Thomassen 2010).

2 The absence of a European *demos* is a major concern of the academic debate on democracy in the EU. The point is, however, that the mechanisms necessary to create a *demos* in Europe are simply not present (see Cederman 2001; Decker 2002).

3 See Scharpf (2002), who identified this issue early and with his usual prescience. Two ECJ rulings in 2007, in the *Viking* and *Laval* cases, have created decisive legal precedents with regard to trade union activity in the EU. Both referred to posted workers, that is, workers from one EU country being employed in another but under

terms and conditions of the former, which were generally worse. The ECJ recognized the right of trade unions to collective action against such practices, but found that this right cannot infringe the freedom to provide services in the EU, that is, to the underpinnings of the single market. Essentially the ECJ ruled that EU legislation has a bearing on national capital–labour disputes in ways that favour capital (see, Barnard 2008; Hinarejos 2008; Nicol 2011).

4 See Menéndez (2012: 70).

5 See Beck (2013) for a thorough discussion of this paradox.

6 See Menéndez (2017) for a detailed account of using the law in the course of the crisis to turn the EU into a 'consolidating' state that manages austerity. European law has been radically altered, opening the gates to authoritarianism. Streeck (2015) made a related point stressing the shift of the EU in the direction of 'authoritarian liberalism' to manage the single market, particularly since the introduction of the euro.

7 On this issue see also Rasmussen (2012), especially in relation to the extra power accruing to the European Parliament.

8 The text of the regulation is available at *http://eur-lex.europa.eu/legal-content/EN/TXT/PDF/?uri=CELEX:320 03R0343&from=EN*.

9 Available at *https://diem25.org/wp-content/uploads/2016/02/diem25_english_long.pdf*.

10 See *http://www.consilium.europa.eu/en/council-eu/voting-system/qualified-majority/*.

11 Indeed the process is even harsher. Regulation (EU) 1173/2011 (available at *https://eur-lex.europa.eu/LexUriServ/LexUriServ.do?uri=OJ:L:2011:306:0001:00 07:en:PDF*), which is part of the Six Pack reforms, introduced so-called 'reverse qualified majority voting'. If a member state is deemed by the Council to have failed

to take action in response to a recommendation by the Council, the Commission can recommend a penalty of lodging an interest-bearing deposit amounting to 0.2% of the member state's GDP in the preceding year. The Commission's recommendation is deemed to be adopted by the Council unless there is a qualified majority to reject it within ten days. For that to happen the minimum required number of votes would be 255 out of a total of 345. Small countries would have absolutely no chance of mustering such majorities.

12 Chrisafis and Rankin (2017).
13 Marx and Engels (1848: 218).
14 Marx and Engels (1848: 241).
15 Riexinger (2017) is a clear example.
16 See Flassbeck and Lapavitsas (2015) and Lapavitsas, Mariolis, and Gavrielidis (2017) for discussion and further readings.
17 There is extensive economic work by post-Keynesians along these lines, including for the USA (see, e.g., Onaran, Stockhammer and Grafl (2011).
18 See Lapavitsas (2013: ch. 7).
19 For detailed empirical work that broadly confirms this point, see Clarke, Goodwin, and Whiteley (2017).

References

Aliber, R.Z. 2010. 'The Devaluation of the Greek Euro', International Political Economy, Special Report, pp. 1–3, 17 February.

Anderson, P. 2010. *The New World Order*, London: Verso.

Argyroulis, D. 2017. '"An Opportunity to Enhance the Cohesion of the Eurozone?" The Greek Sovereign Debt Crisis as a Negative Lesson', paper presented at the UACES 47th Conference, Krakow, Poland, 4–6 September, available at: *http://www.uaces.org/events/conferences/krakow/papers/abstract.php?paper_id=456#.Wjo7qN-gLIU*

Artavanis, N., A. Morse, and M. Tsoutsoura 2012. 'Tax Evasion Across Industries: Soft Credit Evidence from Greece', NBER Working Paper No. 21552, issued in September 2015, available in earlier form at: *https://www.chicagobooth.edu/blogs/informingreform/docs/taxevasion.pdf*

Baldwin, R. and F. Giavazzi (eds) 2015. *The Eurozone Crisis: A Consensus View of the Causes and a Few Possible Solutions*, VoxEU.org Book, London: CEPR Press.

References

Barnard, C. 2008. 'Social Dumping or Dumping Socialism?', *Cambridge Law Journal*, 67(2): 262–4.

Baun, M. 1995–6. 'The Maastricht Treaty as High Politics: Germany, France, and European Integration', *Political Science Quarterly*, Winter, 110(4): 605–24.

Beck, G. 2013. *The Legal Reasoning of the Court of Justice of the EU*, Oxford: Hart Publishing.

Benassi C. and L. Dorigatti 2015. 'Straight to the Core – Explaining Union Responses to the Casualization of Work: The IG Metall Campaign for Agency Workers', *British Journal of Industrial Relations*, 53(3): 533–55.

Bickerton, C.J., D. Hodson, and U. Puetter 2015. 'The New Intergovernmentalism: European Integration in the Post-Maastricht Era', *Journal of Common Market Studies*, 53(4): 703–22.

Bispinck R. and T. Schulten 2011. 'Trade Union Responses to Precarious Employment in Germany', WSI-Diskussionspapier, Nr. 178, The Institute of Economic and Social Research (WSI), Hans Boeckler Foundation, available at: *https://www.boeckler.de/pdf/p_wsi_disp_178.pdf*

Blanchard, O. and D. Leigh 2013. 'Growth Forecast Errors and Fiscal Multipliers', IMF Working Paper WP//13/1, available at *https://www.imf.org/external/pubs/ft/wp/2013/wp1301.pdf*

Blyth, M. 2013. *Austerity: The History of a Dangerous Idea*, New York: Oxford University Press.

Bonefeld, W. 1998. 'Politics of European Monetary Union: Class, Ideology and Critique', *Economic and Political Weekly*, 33(35), 29 Aug.–4 Sept., pp. PE55–69.

Bonefeld, W. 2001. 'European Monetary Union: Ideology and Class', in W. Bonefeld (ed.), *The Politics of Europe: Monetary Union and Class*, Basingstoke: Palgrave Macmillan, pp. 1–9.

Bonefeld, W. 2012. 'Freedom and the Strong State: On German Ordoliberalism', *New Political Economy*, 15(5): 633–56.

Bonefeld, W. 2017. *The Strong State and the Free Economy*, London: Rowman & Littlefield.

Boonstra, W.W. 2010. 'The Creation of a Common European Bond Market', *Cahier Comte Boël*, No. 14, European League for Economic Cooperation, available at *http://www.eleclece.eu/en/system/files/publica tions/cahier-boel/the-creation-of-a-european-comm on-bond-market/b14.pdf*

Böwer, U., V. Michou, and C. Ungerer 2014. 'The Puzzle of the Missing Greek Exports', European Commission, Directorate-General for Economic and Financial Affairs, Economic Papers 518, available at: *http://ec.europa.eu/economy_finance/publications/ economic_paper/2014/pdf/ecp518_en.pdf*

Buchheit, L. and M. Gulati 2010. 'How to Restructure Greek Debt', Duke Law School Working Paper, available at: *http://papers.ssrn.com/sol3/papers.cfm? abstract_id=1603304*

Buck, T. and G. Chazan 2017. 'Martin Schulz Calls for "United States of Europe"', *Financial Times*, 7 December, available at: *https://www.ft.com/content/ ec2a8982-db4a-11e7-a039-c64b1c09b482*

Bugaric, B. 2013. 'Europe Against the Left? On Legal Limits to Progressive Politics', LSE 'Europe in Question' Discussion Paper Series, LEQS Paper No. 61/2013, May, available at: *http://www.lse.ac.uk/ europeanInstitute/LEQS%20Discussion%20Paper %20Series/LEQSPaper61.pdf*

References

Buiter, W., G. Corsetti, and N. Roubini 1993. 'Excessive Deficits: Sense and Nonsense in the Treaty of Maastricht', *Economic Policy*, 8(16): 57–100.

Bulmer, S. 2014. 'Germany and the Eurozone Crisis: Between Hegemony and Domestic Politics', *West European Politics*, 37(6): 1244–63.

Burda M. and J. Hunt 2011. 'What Explains the German Labor Market Miracle in the Great Recession?', Brookings Papers on Economic Activity, 42(1): 273–335, available at: *https://www.brookings.edu/wp-content/uploads/2011/03/2011a_bpea_burda.pdf*

Caliendo M. and J. Hogenacker 2012. 'The German Labor Market after the Great Recession: Successful Reforms and Future Challenges', IZA Discussion Paper No. 6810, August, available at: *http://ftp.iza.org/dp6810.pdf*

Callinicos, A. 2015. 'The Internationalist Case Against the European Union', *International Socialism*, 148, available at *http://isj.org.uk/the-internationalist-case-against-the-european-union/*

Calvo, G. 2007. 'Crises in Emerging Market Economies: A Global Perspective', NBER Working Paper No. 11305, April. Published by the Central Bank of Chile.

Calvo, G., A. Izquierdo, and E. Talvi 2006. 'Phoenix Miracles in Emerging Markets: Recovering without Credit from Systemic Financial Crises', Technical Report, National Bureau of Economic Research.

Caporaso, J.A. 1998. 'Regional Integration Theory: Understanding Our Past and Anticipating Our Future', *Journal of European Public Policy*, 5(1): 1–16.

Caporaso, J.A. and J.T.S. Keeler 1995. 'The European Union and Regional Integration Theory', in C. Rhodes and S. Mazey (eds), *The State of the European Union: Building a European Polity?* Boulder, CO: Lynne Rienner & Company, pp. 29–62.

Cederman, L.-E. 2001. 'Nationalism and Bounded Integration: What It Would Take to Construct a European Demos', *European Journal of International Relations*, 7(2): 139–74.

Cesaratto S. and A. Stirati 2010. 'Germany and the European and Global Crises', *International Journal of Political Economy*, 39(4): 56–86.

Chrisafis, A. and J. Rankin 2017. 'Macron Lays Out Vision for "Profound" Changes in Post-Brexit EU', *The Guardian*, 26 September, available at: *https://www.theguardian.com/world/2017/sep/26/profound-transfor mation-macron-lays-out-vision-for-post-brexit-eu*

Clarke H., M. Goodwin, and P. Whiteley 2017. *Brexit: Why Britain Voted to Leave the European Union*, Cambridge: Cambridge University Press.

Darvas, Z. and S. Merler 2013. 'The European Central Bank in the Age of Banking Union', 1 Policy Contribution, October, Bruegel, Brussels, available at: *http://bruegel.org/2013/10/the-european-central-bank-in-the-age-of-banking-union/*

De Grauwe, P. 2011. 'A Less Punishing, More Forgiving Approach to the Debt Crisis in the Eurozone', Centre for European Policy Studies Brief No. 230, January, available at: *https://www.ceps.eu/system/files/book/2011/01/Policy%20Brief%20No%20230%20De%20Gra uwe%20on%20Debt%20Punishment.pdf*

Decker, F. 2002. 'Governance Beyond the Nation-State: Reflections on the Democratic Deficit of the European Union', *Journal of European Public Policy*, 9(2): 256–72.

References

Delpla, J. and J. von Weizsäcker 2010. 'The Blue Bond Proposal', Bruegel Policy Briefs 420, Bruegel, Brussels, available at: *http://bruegel.org/wp-content/uploads/imported/publications/1005-PB-Blue_Bonds.pdf*

Di Carlo, D. 2018. 'Does Pattern Bargaining Explain Wage Restraint in the German Public Sector?' Max Planck Institute for the Study of Societies, Discussion Paper 18/3, available at: *http://www.mpifg.de/pu/mpifg_dp/2018/dp18-3.pdf*

Dyson, K. 1994. *Elusive Union: The Process of Economic and Monetary Union in Europe*, London: Longman.

Dyson, K. 2000. *The Politics of the Euro-Zone: Stability or Breakdown?* Oxford: Oxford University Press.

Eichengreen, B. 1993. 'European Monetary Unification', *Journal of Economic Literature*, 31(3): 1321–57.

European Commission 2011. *Quarterly Report on the Euro Area*, Vol. 10, No. 3, available at: *http://ec.europa.eu/economy_finance/publications/qr_euro_area/2011/pdf/qrea3_en.pdf*

Feldstein, M. 1997. 'The Political Economy of the European Economic and Monetary Union: Political Sources of an Economic Liability', National Bureau of Economic Research Working Paper Series No. 6150, available at: *http://www.nber.org/papers/w6150.pdf*

Fine B., C. Lapavitsas, and J. Pincus (eds) 2001. *Development Policy in the Twenty-first Century: Beyond the Post-Washington Consensus*, London: Routledge.

Flassbeck, H. and C. Lapavitsas 2013. 'The Systemic Crisis of the Euro: True Causes and Effective Therapies', Rosa Luxemburg Stiftung Studien, available at: *http://www.rosalux.de/fileadmin/rls_uploads/pdfs/Studien/Studien_The_systemic_crisis_web.pdf*

References

Flassbeck, H. and C. Lapavitsas 2015. *Against the Troika: Crisis and Austerity in the Eurozone*, London and New York: Verso.

Fukuyama, F. 1992. *The End of History and the Last Man*, New York: Free Press.

Fukuyama, F. 2007. 'The History at the End of History', *The Guardian*, 3 April, available at: *https://www.theguardian.com/commentisfree/2007/apr/03/thehistoryattheendofhist*

Giurlando, P. 2016. *Eurozone Politics: Perception and Reality in Italy, the UK, and Germany*, London and New York: Routledge.

Gourinchas P.O., T. Philippon, and D. Vayanos 2016. 'The Analytics of the Greek Crisis', in M. Eichenbaum and J. Parker (eds), *NBER Macroeconomics Annual 2016*, Vol. 3, available at: *http://www.nber.org/papers/w22370.pdf*

Gowan, P. 2009. 'Friedrich von Hayek et la construction de l'Europe néolibérale', *Contretemps*, 4: 81–90.

Gross, S. 2013. 'The German Economy and East-Central Europe: The Development of Intra-Industry Trade from Ostpolitik to the Present', *German Politics and Society*, 31(3): 83–105.

Haas, E. 1958 (1968). *The Uniting of Europe: Political, Social, and Economic Forces, 1950–1957*, Stanford, CA: Stanford University Press.

Haas, E. 1975. 'The Obsolescence of Regional Integration Theory', Research Series No. 25, Berkeley, CA: Center for International Studies.

Hadjiiossif, C. 2017. *European Integration, Germany and the Return of Nationalisms* (in Greek), Athens: Vivliorama.

References

Hanzl-Weiss, D. and M. Landesmann 2016. 'Correcting External Imbalances in the European Economy', Research Report 410, April, The Vienna Institute for International Economic Studies.

Hassel, A. 2014. 'The Paradox of Liberalization – Understanding Dualism and the Recovery of the German Political Economy', *British Journal of Industrial Relations*, 52(1): 57–81.

Hayward, J. (ed.) 1995. *The Crisis of Representation in Europe* (special issue of *West European Politics*), London: Frank Cass.

Hayek, F.A. 1939 (1948). 'The Economic Conditions of Interstate Federalism', reprinted in *Individualism and Economic Order*, Chicago: University of Chicago Press, pp. 255–72.

Hayek, F.A. 1976 (1990). *Denationalisation of Money: The Argument Refined*, 3rd edition, London: The Institute of Economic Affairs.

Heise, A. 2005. 'Has Germany Been Europeanised or Has Europe Become (Too) Germanic?', *Intereconomics*, 40(5): 285–91.

Hien, J. and C. Joerges 2018. 'Dead Man Walking: Current European Interest in the Ordoliberal Tradition', Department of Law Working Papers, LAW 2018/03, European University Institute.

Hinarejos, A. 2008. '*Laval* and *Viking*: The Right to Collective Action versus EU Fundamental Freedoms', *Human Rights Law Review*, 8(4): 714–29.

Hooghe, L. and G. Marks 2009. 'A Postfunctionalist Theory of European Integration: From Permissive Consensus to Constraining Dissensus', *British Journal of Political Science*, 39(1): 1–23.

Höpner, M. 2014. 'Europe Would be Better Off without the Euro', *Labour History*, 55(5): 661–6.

Höpner, M. and M. Lutter 2014. 'One Currency and Many Modes of Wage Formation: Why the Eurozone Is Too Heterogeneous for the Euro', Max Planck Institute for the Study of Societies, Discussion Paper 14/14, available at *http://www.mpifg.de/pu/mpifg_dp/dp14-14.pdf*

Höpner, M. and A. Schäfer 2012. 'Integration among Unequals', Max Planck Institute for the Study of Societies, Discussion Paper 12/5, available at *http://www.mpifg.de/pu/mpifg_dp/dp12-5.pdf*

International Monetary Fund 2013. 'German–Central European Supply Chain – Cluster Report', IMF Multi Country Report No. 13/263, August, available at: *https://www.imf.org/en/Publications/CR/Issues/2016/12/31/German-Central-European-Supply-Chain-Cluster-Report-Staff-Report-First-Background-Note-40881*

International Monetary Fund 2016. 'The IMF and the Crises in Greece, Ireland and Portugal: An Evaluation by the Independent Evaluation Office', July, available at: *http://www.ieo-imf.org/ieo/files/completedevaluations/EAC__REPORT%20v5.PDF*

Ioannou, D., P. Leblond, and A. Niemann 2015. 'European Integration and the Crisis: Practice and Theory', *Journal of European Public Policy*, 22(2): 155–76.

James, H. 2012. *Making the European Monetary Union*, Cambridge, MA: Harvard University Press.

Katsimi, M. and T. Moutos 2010. 'EMU and the Greek Crisis: The Political-Economy Perspective', *European Journal of Political Economy*, 26: 568–76.

Katsinos, A. and T. Mariolis 2012. 'Switch to Devalued Drachma and Cost-Push Inflation: A Simple Input–

Output Approach to the Greek Case', *Modern Economy*, 3: 164–70.

Kostis, C. 2015. *The Spoiled Children of History* (in Greek), Athens: Patakis.

Kyriakidis, A. 2016. 'The Greek Crisis 2009–2015: A Comprehensive Analysis of the EU–IMF Financial Assistance Programs', *International Journal of Employment Studies*, 24(2): 7–35.

Landesmann M. and D. Hanzl-Weiss 2013. 'Structural Adjustment and Unit Labour Cost Developments in Europe's Periphery: Patterns Before and During the Crisis', Research Report 390, September, The Vienna Institute for International Economic Studies.

Landesmann M. and S. Leitner (in collaboration with R. Stehrer) 2015. 'Competitiveness of the European Economy', Research Report 401, May, The Vienna Institute for International Economic Studies.

Lapavitsas, C. 2013. *Profiting without Producing: How Finance Exploits Us All*, London and New York: Verso.

Lapavitsas, C. 2017. 'A Socialist Strategy for Europe', *Catalyst*, 1(3), available at: *https://catalyst-journal. com/vol1/no3/a-socialist-strategy-for-europe*

Lapavitsas, C. 2018. 'Political Economy of the Greek Crisis', *Review of Radical Political Economics*, forthcoming.

Lapavitsas, C., A. Kaltenbrunner, D. Lindo, J. Michell, J.P. Painceira, E. Pires, J. Powell, A. Stenfors, and N. Teles 2010a. 'Eurozone Crisis: Beggar Thyself and Thy Neighbour', RMF Occasional Report, March, available at: *http://erensep.org/2010/03/24/first-rmf-report-on-the-eurozone-crisis-beggar-thyself-and-thy-neighbour/#more-146*

References

Lapavitsas, C., A. Kaltenbrunner, G. Lambrinidis, D. Lindo, J. Meadway, J. Michell, J.P. Painceira, E. Pires, J. Powell, A. Stenfors, and N. Teles 2010b. 'The Eurozone between Austerity and Default', RMF Occasional Report, September, available at: *http:// erensep.org/2010/09/24/second-rmf-report-on-the-eurozone-crisis-eurozone-between-austerity-and-de fault/#more-145*

Lapavitsas, C., A. Kaltenbrunner, G. Lambrinidis, D. Lindo, J. Meadway, J. Michell, J.P. Painceira, E. Pires, J. Powell, A. Stenfors, N. Teles, and L. Vatikiotis 2012. *Crisis in the Eurozone*, London and New York: Verso.

Lapavitsas C., T. Mariolis, and C. Gavrielidis 2017. 'Eurozone Failure, German Policies, and a New Path for Greece: Policy Analysis and Proposals', Rosa Luxemburg Stiftung Publikationen, January, available at: *http://eprints.soas.ac.uk/25435/1/lapavitsas-mari olis-3-17-Online-Publ-EurozoneFailure-Web.pdf*

Lapavitsas, C. and D. Munevar 2014. 'Greece Needs a Deep Debt Write-Off', RMF Occasional Policy Paper, 10, available at: *http://archive.economonitor.com/ blog/2014/06/greece-needs-a-deep-debt-write-off/*

Lapavitsas C. and J. Powell 2013. 'Financialisation Varied: A Comparative Analysis of Developed Economies', *Cambridge Journal of Regions, Economy and Society*, 6(3): 359–79.

Mair, P. and J. Thomassen 2010. 'Political Representation and Government in the European Union', *Journal of European Public Policy*, 17(1): 20–35.

Marcussen, M. 1999. 'The Dynamics of EMU Ideas', *Cooperation and Conflict*, 34(4): 383–411.

Mariolis, T. 2013. 'Currency Devaluation, External Finance and Economic Growth: A Note on the

Greek Case', *Social Cohesion and Development*, 8: 59–64.

Mariolis, T. 2016. 'The Foreign-Trade Leakages in the Greek Economy', paper presented at the workshop: 'What is the future for Europe?' of the European Research Network on Social and Economic Policy, AUTh., 26–7 April.

Marks G., L. Hooghe, and K. Blank 1996. 'European Integration from the 1980s: State-Centric v. Multi-level Governance', *Journal of Common Market Studies*, 34(3): 341–78.

Marx K. 1867 (1976). *Capital*, Vol. 1, London: Penguin/ New Left Review.

Marx, K. and F. Engels 1848 (1967). *The Communist Manifesto*, London: Penguin.

McNamara K. and E. Jones 1996. 'The Clash of Institutions: Germany in European Monetary Affairs', *German Politics and Society*, 14(3): 5–30.

Menéndez, A. 2012. 'A Proportionate Constitution? Economic Freedoms, Substantive Constitutional Choices and *Dérapages* in European Union Law', in E. Chiti, A. Menéndez, and P. Teixeira (eds), *The European Rescue of the European Union?* ARENA Report No 3/12, RECON Report No 19, Centre for European Studies, University of Oslo, pp. 69–156, available at: *https://pure.au.dk/ws/files/69770796/ RECONreport1912.pdf*

Menéndez, A. 2017. 'The Crisis of Law and the European Crises: From the Social and Democratic *Rechtsstaat* to the Consolidating State of (Pseudo-)technocratic Governance', *Journal of Law and Society*, 44(1): 56–78.

Merler, S. and J. Pisani-Ferry 2012. 'Sudden Stops in

the Euro Area', Policy Contribution, March, Bruegel, Brussels, available at: *http://bruegel.org/wp-con tent/uploads/imported/publications/pc_2012_06. pdf*

Milward, A. 1994. *The European Rescue of the Nation State*, London: Routledge.

Moravscik, A. 1991. 'Negotiating the Single European Act: National Interests and Conventional Statecraft in the European Community', *International Organisation*, 45(1): 19–56.

Moravscik, A. 1993. 'Preferences and Power in the European Community: A Liberal Intergovermentalist Approach', *Journal of Common Market Studies*, 31(4): 473–524.

Moravscik, A. 1998. *The Choice for Europe: Social Purpose and State Power from Messina to Maastricht*, Ithaca, NY: Cornell University Press; and London: Routledge.

Mundell, R.A. 1961. 'A Theory of Optimum Currency Areas', *American Economic Review*, 51(4): 657–65.

Negri, T. 2005. 'Oui, pour faire disparaître cette merde d'État-nation', interview in *Libération*, 13 May, available at: *http://www.liberation.fr/france/2005/05/13/ oui-pour-faire-disparaitre-cette-merde-d-etat-nation_ 519624*

Nicol, D. 2011. 'Europe's Lochner Moment', *Public Law*, 2(April): 307–28.

Nikiforos, M., D. Papadimitriou, and G. Zezza 2016. 'The Greek Public Debt Problem', Working Paper No. 867, Levy Economics Institute of Bard College, May, available at: *http://www.levyinstitute.org/pubs/ wp_867.pdf*

Norris, P. 1997. 'Representation and the Democratic

Deficit', *European Journal of Political Research*, 32: 273–82.

Onaran, Ö., E. Stockhammer, and L. Grafl, 2011. 'Financialisation, Income Distribution and Aggregate Demand in the USA', *Cambridge Journal of Economics*, 35(4): 637–61.

Pisani-Ferry, J. 2011. *The Euro Crisis and Its Aftermath*, Oxford: Oxford University Press.

Pisani-Ferry, J., A. Sapir, and G. Wolff 2013. 'EU–IMF Assistance to Euro-Area Countries: An Early Assessment', *Blueprint 19*, Brussels: Bruegel.

Polanyi, K. 1944 (2001). *The Great Transformation*, Boston: Beacon Press.

Rasmussen, A. 2012. 'Twenty Years of Co-decision since Maastricht: Inter- and Intrainstitutional Implications', *European Integration*, 34(7): 735–51.

Reho, F.O. 2017. 'The Past and Future of European Federalism: Spinelli vs. Hayek', briefing published at EPICENTER, Wilfried Martens Center for European Studies, available at: *https://www.martenscentre.eu/sites/default/files/publication-files/european-federalism-spinelli-hayek.pdf*

Riexinger, B. 2017. 'Illusions of EU Exit', *Catalyst*, 1(3), available at: *https://catalyst-journal.com/vol1/no3/illusions-of-eu-exit*

Rocholl, J. and A. Stahmer 2016. 'Where Did the Greek Bailout Money Go?' ESMT White Paper No. WP–16–02, Berlin: European School of Management and Technology, available at: *http://static.esmt.org/publications/whitepapers/WP-16-02.pdf*

Ruoff, B. 2016. 'Labour Market Developments in Germany: Tales of Decency and Stability', Working Paper No. 39, International Labour Office; Global

References

Labour University, Geneva, available at: *http://www.global-labour-university.org/fileadmin/GLU_Working_Papers/GLU_WP_No.39.pdf*

Saad-Filho A. and D. Johnston 2005. *Neoliberalism: A Critical Reader*, London and Ann Arbor, MI: Pluto Press.

Samuelson, P. and W. Barnett (eds) 2007. *Inside the Economist's Mind: Conversations with Eminent Economists*. Oxford: Blackwell.

Scharpf, F. 2002. 'The European Social Model', *Journal of Common Market Studies*, 40(4): 645–70.

Scharpf, F. 2006. 'Problem Solving Effectiveness and Democratic Accountability in the EU', Institute for Advanced Studies, Vienna, 107, Political Science Series, available at: *http://aei.pitt.edu/6097/1/pw_107.pdf*

Scharpf, F. 2010. *Community and Autonomy: Institutions, Policies and Legitimacy in Multilevel Europe*, Publication Series of the Max Planck Institute for the Study of Societies, Cologne, Germany, Vol. 68, Frankfurt and New York: Campus Verlag, available at: *http://www.mpifg.de/pu/mpifg_book/mpifg_bd_68.pdf*

Scharpf, F. 2011. 'Monetary Union, Fiscal Crisis and the Preemption of Democracy', MPIfG Discussion Paper 16/15, available at: *http://www.mpifg.de/pu/mpifg_dp/dp11-11.pdf*

Scharpf, F. 2016. 'Forced Structural Convergence in the Eurozone – Or a Differentiated European Monetary Community', MPIfG Discussion Paper 16/15, available at: *http://www.mpifg.de/pu/mpifg_dp/dp16-15.pdf*

Sheehan, H. 2017. *The Syriza Wave: Surging and*

Crashing with the Greek Left, New York: NYU Press.

Sinn, H.W. 2014. 'Austerity, Growth and Inflation: Remarks on the Eurozone's Unresolved Competitiveness Problem', *The World Economy*, 37(1): 1–13.

Skaperdas, S. 2011. 'Seven Myths about the Greek Debt Crisis', UC Irvine Working Paper, October, available at: *http://www.socsci.uci.edu/~sskaperd/SkaperdasMythsWP1011.pdf*

Smits, R. 1996. 'The European Central Bank: Institutional Aspects', *The International and Comparative Law Quarterly*, 45(2): 319–42.

Sotiris, P. 2018. 'Gramsci and the Challenges for the Left: The Historical Bloc as a Strategic Concept', *Science & Society*, 82(1): 94–119.

Stiglitz, J. 2016. *The Euro: How a Common Currency Threatens the Future of Europe*, New York: W.W. Norton.

Stockhammer, E. 2008. 'Some Stylized Facts on the Finance-Dominated Accumulation Regime', *Competition and Change*, 12(2): 184–202.

Storm, S. and C.W.M. Naastepad 2015. 'NAIRU Economics and the Eurozone Crisis', *International Review of Applied Economics*, 29(6): 843–77.

Streeck, W. 2014. *Buying Time: The Delayed Crisis of Democratic Capitalism*, London and New York: Verso.

Streeck, W. 2015. 'Heller, Schmitt and the Euro', *European Law Journal*, 21(3): 361–70.

Streeck, W. 2016. *How Will Capitalism End?* London and New York: Verso.

Torres, F. 2007. 'The Long Road to EMU: The Economic

and Political Reasoning behind Maastricht', Working Papers in Economics, 50, Universidade de Aveiro.

Tsipouri, L. 2015. *European Economic Integration* (in Greek), Athens: National Documentation Centre, University of Athens.

Tuori, K. 2016. 'Has Euro Area Monetary Policy Become Redistribution by Monetary Means? "Unconventional" Monetary Policy as a Hidden Transfer Mechanism', *European Law Journal*, 22(6): 838–68.

Varoufakis, Y. 2017. *Adults in the Room: My Battle with Europe's 'Deep Establishment'*, London: Penguin Random House.

Vavouras, I. 2013. *Economic Policy* (in Greek), Athens: Papazisis.

Verdun, A. 1999. 'The Role of the Delors Committee in the Creation of EMU: An Epistemic Community?', *Journal of European Public Policy*, 6(2): 308–28.

Wagner, I. 2015. 'Rule Enactment in a Pan-European Labour Market: Transnational Posted Work in the German Construction Sector', *British Journal of Industrial Relations*, 53(4): 692–710.

Webber, D. 2014. 'How Likely Is It That the European Union Will Disintegrate? A Critical Analysis of Competing Theoretical Perspectives', *European Journal of International Relations*, 20(2): 341–65.

Weiler, J.H.H. 2012. 'In the Face of Crisis: Input Legitimacy, Output Legitimacy and the Political Messianism of European Integration', *European Integration* 34(7): 825–41.

Weiler, J.H.H., U. Haltern, and F. Mayer 1995. 'European Democracy and Its Critique', *West*

European Politics, 18(3): 4–39 (special issue on 'The Crisis of Representation in Europe').

Wyplosz, C. 2006. 'European Monetary Union: The Dark Sides of a Major Success', *Economic Policy*, 21(46): 209–61.

Wyplosz, C. and S. Sgherri 2016. 'The IMF's Role in Greece in the Context of the 2010 Stand-By Arrangement', Independent Evaluation Office Background Paper, BP/16-02/11, available at: *http:// www.ieo-imf.org/ieo/files/completedevaluations/EA C__BP_16-02_11__The_IMFs_Role_in_Greece_in_ the_Context_of_the_2010_SBA.PDF*

Yamamura K. and W. Streeck 2003. *The End of Diversity? Prospects for German and Japanese Capitalism*, Ithaca, NY: Cornell University Press.

Zettelmeyer, J., C. Trebesch, and M. Gulati 2013. 'The Greek Debt Restructuring: An Autopsy', *Economic Policy*, 28(75): 513–63.

Zielonka, J. 2018. *Counter-Revolution: Liberal Europe in Retreat*, Oxford: Oxford University Press.

Index

Index

Index

Index

179

Index

Index

Index

Index